My Guru,

To: Jason
For your long-standing contribution
to my Aunt and friends
somehow [illegible] as well as wonted
[illegible] Kingsley

London
5/12/13

MY GURU, SRI CHINMOY

LIFE AND TEACHINGS

MANATITA

Vajra Books
www.vajrabooks.com.np

Published & Distributed by
Vajra Books
Jyatha, Thamel, Kathmandu, Nepal
Tel.: 977-1-4220562, Fax: 977-1-4246536
e-mail: bidur_la@mos.com.np
www.vajrabooks.com.np

ISBN 978-9937-623-04-9

Printed in Nepal

Sri Chinmoy

Contents

Foreword

I write these few words just as the great feast of sport at the London Olympiad is coming to a close. Somehow it seems a suitable backdrop against which to situate a Spiritual Master who, as Manatita tells us in this beautiful volume of personal reminiscences, was so taken with the links between the physical and the spiritual. No mean sportsman himself, Śri Chinmoy was a great teacher and a great friend to politicians and Olympians alike, from Nelson Mandela to Carl Lewis. What was his secret?

These pages tell me that the glory of human beings is an incredible capacity to mirror the very life of God. Every now and then we get a glimpse of what is possible – in amazing feats of athletic accomplishment, of course, but also in ordinary yet often heroic acts of kindness and courage. We all need leaders who can show us the way – and Manatita has written warmly of his hero in these pages. But it's all too easy for us to become passive spectators, admirers from afar. The best of teachers does not act like some super-nanny, keeping us secure but isolated and all too comfortable. The secret of the good teacher - fairly obvious really - is to know how to challenge, to bring the best out of the pupil.

My own inspiration is not Śri Chinmoy, however much I may respect him, but a 16thCentury Spanish priest called Ignatius of Loyola. I think he and Śri Chinmoy would have enjoyed each other's company. Ignatius began his little book of Spiritual Exercises by saying that 'as strolling, walking and running are bodily exercises, so every way of preparing and disposing the soul to rid itself of all the disordered tendencies, and, after it is rid, to seek and find the Divine Will is called a Spiritual Exercise.' The physical and the spiritual are all of a piece. It takes time to learn how to co-operate with the grace which comes from God. But to those with the deepest of desires, and who have the fortune to know a good teacher, it is a gift which is always granted.

– Dr. Michael Barnes SJ.
5th September, 2012.

Preview

In his book, *My Guru, Sri Chinmoy: Life And Teachings*, Manatita demonstrates most admirably, the spirit of love, of sweetness, simplicity and power. He also conveys to the fullest, Sri Chinmoy's unconditional love for the Supreme: God the Creator; God the Creation. Manatita tells us – through the teachings of his Guru - that all things sentient and insentient are part and parcel of the Supreme, and that, "whatever takes place in the divine Providence is not only for the best, but also inevitable, because there is no alternative." - Sri Chinmoy. (*Eternity's Breath*, (1972), Agni Press). In short, God is the only Doer.

A theme running through most of this book is Sri Chinmoy's timeless message of living in the Eternal Now, the Sacrament of the Present Moment. Here one also encounters Sri Chinmoy's unique teachings on not wasting time; of God not being bound by plans; the importance of physical fitness; the concept of Self- Transcendence, and the Guru's emphasis on speed. Indeed Sri Chinmoy did everything with tremendous speed, and never wasted a moment.

Sri Chinmoy's powerful legacy shows how his lofty teachings have reached and touched the lives of millions. Through his many and varied manifestations which include literature, music, sport, art, weight-lifting and several other initiatives, numerous souls have been inspired to go beyond themselves; to transcend barriers standing in their way. We see that a significant number came from the world of luminaries, Presidents, celebrities, athletes and politicians, as well as eminent spiritual leaders across the religious spectrum.

Sri Chinmoy brought down from Heaven a current day message of love of Truth; of world acceptance and transformation, while maintaining one's one-pointed devotion to God. He advocated prayer, meditation and the spirit of selfless service to the Supreme in humanity. He travelled to numerous countries, spreading his message of inner peace through music and many other inspirational mediums. Sri Chinmoy was so prolific and such an exemplary person, that he was admired and adored by many as the 21st century's first global man.

Manatita invites us to walk with him, as he travels through the pages of this sacred work. We see his sweet simplicity and shining spirit; as well as his love for God and later Sri Chinmoy. As Manatita develops into a happy village boy growing up in the Caribbean, one is touched by his description of village life; his Christian influence and love for Christ, and finally his re-awakening into the life Divine in London, UK, a distant country and away from home.

He immerses us through a poetic and heart-rending piece of prose, *The Prologue,* an account of the Mahasamadhi – a God-man's conscious exit from this world – of Sri Chinmoy. This is perhaps the most powerful and moving of all chapters written here. Manatita continues to write with great clarity and candour on spiritual transformation; adapting to changes that come with devotion to God, and embellishes it with the joy of inner experiences.

Finally, Manatita describes Sri Chinmoy's early life, some aspects of what may have later fashioned his Guru's personality and character; his vision, and his core teachings of Love, Devotion and Surrender, as described in chapters 11 and 12. Manatita concludes with a look at the Master's powerful legacy to his disciples and to humanity at large.

This book is full of love, light, wisdom and clarity. It is a great source of inspiration and an invaluable help to me. I trust that you, too, his readers, find in these pages, a fountain of knowledge and an insightful guide towards your journey of Self-discovery.

–Thomas McGuire. Writer.
16th September, 2012.

Author's Note

On July 22, 1966 in Santurce, Puerto Rico, the first Sri Chinmoy Centre - initially called the AUM Centre - was inaugurated. Soon afterwards, a Centre was established in New York where Sri Chinmoy was based, in Jamaica, Queens. It is still the main venue where disciples meet for their tri-annual celebrations. Sri Chinmoy has since travelled the globe, from North and South America to the Caribbean; to Europe, (East and West) Africa, Asia and Australasia; to include Japan and China also. There are over 160 Sri Chinmoy Centres in more than 60 countries around the globe.

Now officially the Sri Chinmoy Centre Church, it is generally referred to as the Sri Chinmoy Centre, or occasionally Sri Chinmoy Centre International. A worldwide organisation, it is perhaps the most powerful legacy founded by Sri Chinmoy. It is the medium through which all other initiatives and activities as encouraged by Sri Chinmoy, takes place, and many are mentioned towards the ending of this book. The Sri Chinmoy Centre seeks to exemplify the Master's teachings by the propagation of inner and outer peace through prayer and meditation, and initiatives in sports, music, literature, drama, poetry and art, humanitarian projects and many other creative and positive ideas.

"Sri Chinmoy," "Master," "Guru," or "Guruji," are simply different words for the same person: Sri Chinmoy. We, his disciples, mostly address or refer to him lovingly and affectionately as "Guru."

I feel extremely fortunate and get a tremendous sense of divine pride in being a disciple of Sri Chinmoy. Sometimes, and seemingly in the smallest things, as well as other aspects of the Master's work, I experience a powerful inner thrill and great jubilation within my Soul. This inner sublimity brings with it a profound reverence; an indescribable inner beauty, gratitude and a prayer for God's victory, humanity's victory, here on earth as well as in heaven.

It is my fervent hope that I can share this sacredness, this sanctity; this love - for this is really what it is - with you, my reader, throughout the pages of this book. In this way, I can continue to serve the Master, my Guruji, and My Supreme ... my all. I trust you find it useful.

Dedication
and
Acknowledgements

This book is inspired by my Spiritual Teacher, Sri Chinmoy, a remarkable and unprecedented human being, whom I intend to introduce to you in the following chapters. I became a student of Sri Chinmoy on the 1st of October 1982. I give Sri Chinmoy all credit for the Light which I embody today, for he has shaped and is continuing to mould my inner and outer life even now, five years after his Mahasamadhi – a God-man's conscious exit from this earthly plane.

My acknowledgements to Hridananda, my fellow Gurubhai – a direct disciple of Sri Chinmoy - who has continuously and self-givingly helped me with this book. I have made many positive changes and additions, due to his invaluable and loving advice; To Elsie Mack, an 89-year old woman, who has most diligently and soulfully assisted me with the proof-reading. Finally, to Dora Withers, an extremely dear friend, who has also read my work and made invaluable suggestions.

My deepest and most heart-felt love to Dhiraja Barnaby Mc Bryde, who gave me ceaseless hours of his loving service; Pavitrata Taylor, Kedar Misani, Niriha, Prashphutita, Dipavajan, Parichayaka and courtesy of *www.srichinmoyphotos.com, (Last visited 21st October, 2012.)* for the use of the photographs in this book. My *pranams* to Thomas McGuire, Adam Thornton, Shivaram Trichur, Savvyasachi Brown, Tejvan Pettinger, Dr Michael Barnes and others, who have most soulfully helped towards this noble cause of service. Finally, a soulful bow to the esteemed Pir Zia Vilayat Khan, Head of Sufi International, for his loving endorsement of the book.

This book is written as a labour of love, with reverence; with a selfless spirit of soulful offering. I have tried my best to be objective, precise and as sincere as I can be. Spiritual Masters come to serve Mankind, and I do not wish for Sri Chinmoy to be confined to any boxes. Men and women of God come to serve humanity. I am extremely happy to be given the capacity to play a minor part.

This book is dedicated to God-lovers and God-seekers everywhere. The Master wrote extensively, and his literary works can be found in numerous libraries and in bookstores around the world. This link is just one of them *www.srichinmoylibrary.org*. This is but a humble and tiny glimpse of the infinite source and fullness-reservoir which is Sri Chinmoy, and his message to the modern world. I trust you find it useful and uplifting.

- Manatita 16th March, 2012.

The Invocation

"This prayer embodies the meaning of our path. We did not create this prayer, but God created it so he could teach us how to pray to him."
Comment at Lake Atitlan, Guatemala. December 18th, 1997. - *Sri Chinmoy.*
(Cited in A Day in The Life Of A Sri Chinmoy Disciple, Page 10, (2008), Agni Press*)*

"Once a day you should sing the Invocation. If you don't sing the Invocation once a day, please feel that something is missing in your life. For that day you are not feeding the Supreme; and if you don't feed the Supreme every day, it is an unpardonable crime. The Supreme is not going to give you a mark if you cannot carry a tune. As long as you sing soulfully, the Supreme will be extremely pleased."

God The Supreme Musician, (1976), Agni Press.

My Dear Brother,

Congratulations with your magnificent book, a real offering of devotion and love to the aspiring soul of humanity and the descending Light of Divinity. The book really stands as a work of art and a spiritual offering on its own solid ground, besides the tremendous value added by your inclusion of so many aspects of Sri Chinmoy's ideology, vision and words.

I feel immensely grateful and honoured to have been able to offer a little bit of my time in accompanying you, along the road of this laudable endeavour.

All my best wishes, in the continuation of your journey.

Your loving Gurubhai - Hridananda.

Prologue:
In Memoriam, Part 1.

Tuesday October 16th, 2007

When I am Gone Away

When I am gone away, Remember me, O children sweet

No, not because I failed, No, not because I cried, No, not because I tried,

No, not because I saw my Lord in you, No, not because I served my Lord in you, No, not because I fulfilled my Lord in you,

No, not because I was your Pilot true,
No, not because I was your 'Infinite' blue,

O but because my life was all gratitude, gratitude, gratitude. To you, to you, my children sweet, to you. - Sri Chinmoy. (*Song composed in 1974*).
Glimpses of The Eternal Friend, p. 125, (2010), Agni Press.

I can still hear the music - vocals, instrumentals – soul-stirringly conveying the sublime beauty of the songs *Akarane Prabhu; Namo Narayan, and My Own Gratitude Heart,* amongst many others. Here at the Aspiration-Ground[1], in magnificent surroundings of a quiet area of Jamaica, Queens, New York, all is serene, peaceful, ethereal, majestic and certainly inspirational. Above the court, and on the bench beneath the tree where I am sitting, I can feel the music floating upwards –flute, harp, cello, synthesizer, violin, piano and others – and permeating the inmost recesses of my being. The Master, Sri Chinmoy, had only recently entered Mahasamadhi, a God-man's conscious exit from this world.

Surrounding the inner perimeter of the Court, one can see Sri Chinmoy's students – men, women and children - dressed in white garments and saris. Some remain standing while others sit. Silent, tearful, prayerful, and with expressions on their faces, which convey the momentous occasion of the Mahasamadhi of Sri Chinmoy, their beloved Guru. With hands folded soulfully, the disciples wait patiently and lovingly, some for as long as five hours, to catch a glimpse of Bhagavan Sri Chinmoy.

Lying "in state", his body resting in tranquillity and repose, in his beautifully decorated Casket, Sri Chinmoy looks the epitome of radiance, even more so as the days go by. This is especially touching, as his body was not embalmed. Thus the Master's body was left to emanate naturally, for days, the very powerful experience of Light, shared by so many assembled there. Moving in and out, hardly noticeable to the general audience, are a few disciple volunteers and other Sri Chinmoy students, diligently preparing the area, and making sure that all is in order for this very special occasion.

The Aspiration-Temple² presents as a pinnacle of holiness, beauty, regality, saintliness, power and serenity. Many candles, all in holders of differing shapes and sizes, adorn its surroundings. They are alight and the lingering fragrance of frankincense, jasmine and other incenses, adds all the more to the sense of a joyful transition from here to a more heavenly abode. Flowers stand almost everywhere, and the powerful images of Mother Kali, Sri Chinmoy's mother Mata Yoga Maya, and other gold-crested decorations, enhance even more the kingly attributes of the main Temple shrine.

Down in the Courtyard, and in full view of the many disciples and devotees who stand prayerfully in line to view their Master's body, is a smaller Shrine. Here again is a ubiquitous and beautiful floral arrangement, gold-plated ornaments, heart-shaped garlands and a striking Transcendental – a picture of Sri Chinmoy taken in a meditative state that his disciples use for meditation – that stands in the middle. My experience upon passing this small meditative Shrine of the Master is certainly a very profound and meaningful peace from deep within.

The perimeter of the Courtyard, and indeed the Aspiration-Ground, is surrounded by overhanging trees, flowers, shrubs, pots and plants of many varieties. They spread out naturally along the edges and inside of the Court, adding to the energy, newness, atmosphere and life of the entire grounds.

It is two days since the last tribute was given from the invited guests: luminaries, athletes, musicians, politicians and ordinary folks. They all came from near and far to express their love for their dear Guruji. It was then that conches blew and heart-felt tributes brought many a tear to numerous eyes. It was also then that incense holders was swung back and forth by others, in homage and obeisance to Sri Chinmoy's passing. Mother Heaven must have been tremendously proud of such a noble Soul of unparalleled goodness and love for God.

The chairs are still there, only occupied by others now. The atmosphere is even more serene, more powerful...still tearful, yet strong. Well into its sixth day, Tuesday October 16th, 2007, the wake and transition of Sri Chinmoy, who has just entered Samadhi, in his 76th year, goes on.

The voice of Sri Chinmoy occasionally sings softly over the speakers, various individuals or instrumental groups still perform their Guru's varied compositions, and even the multi-coloured cart which carried all the beautiful floral arrangements, stands majestically at the door on its two large wheels. For an occasion of such magnitude; such depth, it is only fitting that one ends with the immortal and prophetic message of a poem given by the Guru himself, just one day prior to his passing:

> "My physical death is not the end of my life. I am an eternal journey" –*Sri Chinmoy. My Christmas-New Year-Vacation-Aspiration-Prayers, Part 52, Aph.9, (2007)* Agni Press.

Prologue:
In Memoriam, Part 2

Wednesday 17th October, 2007.

As I walk through the gates of the Aspiration-Ground, I can easily see that the place is different now. Gone are the candles and the walkway leading to the Temple- Shrine. It is now swept clean; disciples are busy working on the smaller Shrine, and the inner perimeter of the Aspiration-Ground. The multi-coloured cart has been moved closer to this Shrine. It is now even more beautiful and houses a miniature temple with a bouquet of flowers on either side. This miniature temple is actually a 'love offering box' discreetly placed so that disciples can gladly donate something to affray the enormous cost of the proceedings.

Many disciples are sitting and waiting, and so it occurs to me that perhaps some kind of announcement will be made soon. Sure enough, about twenty minutes later, Alo Devi[1] enters the Courtyard. A brief announcement is made that Sri Chinmoy's body will be buried soon, and that there will be an opportunity for one last viewing.

Several disciples are now entering this sacred ground. I estimate about twelve to thirteen hundred at full capacity. Others are standing in homage with folded hands, and the silence of the morning at Aspiration-Ground, seems to be impregnated with intense aspiration and goodness of spirit. Slowly, the 'walk past' to the Guru's Temple-Shrine begins, and a long single line of disciples, men, women and children appear, coming forward from different locations. They walk past their Guruji's casket silently and prayerfully for the last time.

The homage being over, the curtains at the entrance to the casket slowly begin to close and once again, the disciples who are by this time back in their seats stand again to pay their last respects. Twenty minutes or so later, the curtains re-open. The casket is now draped in cloth but still open. Slowly the screen closes again.

Just before two o'clock, the curtains open once more. This time the casket shines in all its splendour. A significant difference is that the lid is now closed, and the drape has gone. An announcement is made that the digging for the burial will soon take place, and a tent is erected just in front of Aspiration-Temple for that purpose.

*****

It is a few hours later. The small shrine is even more majestic. Around its perimeter, roughly fourteen feet tall, and marginally wider, is an adornment of lighted candles in tall glass cylindrical shapes. Many flower-garlands of a myriad of beautiful colours are present. They look red, yellow, pink, white, saffron and so forth. There are many baskets of floral arrangements, and the 'Transcendental'[2] picture stands powerfully in the middle of the Shrine. There is a very lofty and stately presence about this Shrine. It has now become the focus for meditation as work continues with the digging behind the tent.

Down in the Courtyard, many disciples are working on a large metal pulley to lift the huge Vault, which has now been brought into the Grounds. Slowly they shift its lid and the Vault is painted white and also limed. Alo Devi arrives, and reads from Guru's book "Death and Reincarnation", for a short while. There is then some singing by German and Austrian disciples and the evening closes with the powerful and hauntingly beautiful sound of the mantra AUM[1].

*****

This morning, Thursday 18th October 2007, as I enter the Courtyard at Aspiration- Ground, the silence, reverence and heavenly charm of the occasion once again send a thrill to my body. The two white, majestic, and divinely proud, sculptured lions remain poised just inside the entrance of the gate. Many disciples are sitting and more are coming in anticipation of the final ceremony. Gone is the Vault that was in the Courtyard. One can still see parts of it from the hole in the ground, which is now exposed. The disciples had inserted the vault during the night. And so this crypt now stands in waiting for the final observances to take place.

A French disciple enters Aspiration-Ground carrying a very large and magnificent bouquet of flowers. It is attached to a wooden sign which says: "Your Oneness-Heart is my Supreme Victory." This aphorism was once given to the French and British disciples. How appropriate it seems now, for all the disciples seem to think and feel as one. Heads bowed or straight, standing or sitting, all are waiting prayerfully and reverently for the unfoldment of the day's event. The fragrance of burning incense lingers, and one can still see a tear or two as the assembled disciples and devotees mourn their Guru's passing.

The ceremony begins at about 12.15 hours. Alo Devi leads the audience, now numbering about 1500 or so, with Sri Chinmoy's "Invocation." It begins with "Supreme, Supreme, Supreme, I bow to Thee, I Bow." This song, needless to say, is sung with folded hands and members stand to pay their respects. Slowly the Casket is carried to the Crypt, while soulful and prayerful songs and melodies waft the atmosphere and permeate the hearts and souls of everyone present. Conches blow and bells ring all around. Some selected disciples salute, while others become Casket-bearers. Amidst it all, a Funeral Director is supervising the proceedings while the Casket is being laid into the ground.

The disciples put some marble sand into the Vault with the Casket, and there follows a slow procession of Sand-bearers as the lid is lowered into the ground. The singing continues...harps; voices, harmoniums... and the burning of frankincense and myrrh give off an enchanting and ethereal fragrance to the audience. The Crypt finally covered, the disciples are invited to walk around their Guruji's resting place once, as a way of paying respect, according to Indian tradition. I gather that it is actually three times, but the devotees and disciples are too many, and so two long-standing disciples of Sri Chinmoy - do it three times in oneness with their brother and sister disciples. All the disciples present also get the opportunity to sprinkle some marble sand at their Guruji's Crypt.

I would like to say that it was a moving tribute and an exquisitely fitting farewell to Maha Avatar Sri Chinmoy. While Adarsha – a singer disciple from Scotland - was singing Guruji's heart-rending and soulfully liberating *Jiban Debata and My Own Gratitude Heart,* surely divine bells and conches would have been ringing in the inner worlds. Golden Chariots would have been busy and trumpets joyfully sounding on the other side. Sri Chinmoy had said that God took the responsibility of his life and would be taking the responsibility of his death. With this awe-inspiring and memorable ceremony, God certainly did. And so it is farewell and parting benedictions, to a most noble and unprecedented Physical Presence, who gave his ALL, to the glory of God in ALL.

-Manatita- Friday 19th, October 2007.

CHAPTER ONE

Tracing My Spiritual Unfoldment

"Whatever takes place in the divine Providence is not only for the best, but also
Inevitable, because there is no alternative."

-*Sri Chinmoy.*
Eternity's Breath, (1972), Agni Press.

Strange, and perhaps remarkable, that I do not remember much of that day in
the spring of 1983, for in my soul it was a most noteworthy evening, and I was
filled with joy. It was in an ordinary-looking high school called PS 86, on the
corner of Parson's Boulevard/Hillside Avenue, Jamaica, Queens, New York,
where I first met Sri Chinmoy. This was one of many such evenings, and I felt
quite happy, at home and at peace.

What I remember most was my meeting with Ashrita, that exuberant
persona of a human being, whom I was to meet numerous times later and
sometimes when I was experiencing a great need in life.What I asked him
then, I do not recall, but perhaps it was about his inner relationship with Sri
Chinmoy. In any case, I remember his short and inspirational answer fairly
well. "I am feeling Him right now, I always do." He said to me, pointing to his
heart.

I joined the Sri Chinmoy Centre on the 1st October, 1982, in London,
and went to New York the following year. This was my first trip to Queens,
NY, and it helped to further cement a conscious and eternal relationship with
my Guru, Sri Chinmoy.

*****

I was born Cecil Kingsley Hutchinson, in a beautiful little village called
Hermitage, in the Parish of St Patrick's, Grenada, West Indies (W.I.). This
wonderful paradise, with its colourful flora and delightful beaches, is still
known as the Isle of Spice and everything nice. Nevertheless, I cannot truly

say that the hurricane, Janet, in 1955, was quite so nice. I was just three years old then, and I believe my auntie sought shelter, while shielding me in her arms, beneath the counter of my grandfather's shop. Away from shelter, the torrential rain, blistering winds and storm raged furiously and continuously outside.

I had a very beautiful childhood. I do not know why it should be so, for my mother had very little money, needed support from others to help bring me up, and was a single 'mom'. She became pregnant while still at school and not quite seventeen. As a consequence of her being so young and with child, she was forced to seek support from elsewhere, as my grandfather was totally unforgiving at that time.

Old Montague, what an honourable yet strict man he was! He worked hard all his life, dabbled at everything and succeeded at nothing, save perhaps a loving relationship with his noble wife – my grandmother - who lived and died with him, both in their seventies. We, the children and grandchildren, loved them both dearly. I was also fond of our devoted dog called Mylo.

I can still remember my joy of going to the lands or 'garden', as we called it, my bathing in the river with other boys, and the telling of Anancy (folklore) stories. This we sometimes did deep into the night, with the cool breeze of the nutmeg, banana and palm trees showering their grace upon us. We were also grateful for the life- force of the pipe water from our bubbling springs, to quench our thirst, throats parched from telling stories for a very long time. To this day I have not tasted water so cool and so life-nourishing.

How I loved those times: the catching of the crayfishes from beneath the river stones, the boys taking it in turns to cook 'steam-down' breadfruit, crayfish and dumplings, crab and callaloo, rice and peas, and other national dishes. We sometimes ate on the same plate, or shared the same dish, and occasionally shared the same bed when having an afternoon nap. We also enjoyed playing marbles in our yard, while we listened to the crowing of the 'cocks' (roosters) from the coop beneath the house. Some forty to forty-five years ago, and in a small country village paradise, we were all so innocent! All the trappings of this modern life were so alien to us!

These reminiscences are part of what I mean by having a very beautiful childhood. Of course we fought as boys would, played cricket, drove recklessly down hills on home-made carts, spun tops, dug for miniature turtles in the ground, and did many other crazy things in the late fifties and early sixties. Down in Grenville, in the Parish of St Andrew's, we played football in the Park, went to late night movies, or could easily be found "liming" on the streets and bridges on a hot day. Throughout all this my mother allowed me freedom, and perhaps I was also a very willing boy. I remember always wanting to go to school, to do good, to help, and to be cheerful.

We were a loving family, but although I was never short of food in what was essentially a small agricultural country, I was the first of seven children and my mother's financial position was never that brilliant, even at the best of times.

My first experiences with spirituality happened quite early. I was brought up an Anglican, and was baptised and confirmed at the age of nine. Like most of my friends, I went to Sunday school, and so I was exposed to the religious life at an early age. During this period some evangelist preachers visited Grenada, and so I followed them to their various locations where they gave talks and preached about the Godly life.

I can still see their enormous marquees in our recreation ground and market places, their makeshift churches and huge tents along our sea front in the city of St. George's, as they sought to save souls and turn them to God. Some of the speakers were extremely inspirational. Needless to say, I followed them everywhere. I was so fired with the love of God! By the time I was thirteen, I had numerous certificates for outstanding biblical studies, and really wanted to have an encounter with Jesus Christ.

School life was great. I went to a private school at four, which was run by 'Teacher Leonoris', as we called her. During this period I was exceptionally bright. When I was five my mother took me to the city of Grenville, St. Andrew's. There she began her search for a better and more fulfilling life. I went to the St. Andrew's Methodist School, experienced morning assemblies, learnt moral principles and said 'grace' before meals. All this greatly helped to shape my spiritual life.

Here I was to stay until I was fifteen. For what were perhaps God-ordained reasons, I did not sit the scholarship exams at nine and again at eleven. Consequently, I did not go to High School. Who knows, had I done so, I may have been a scholarly Professor somewhere, and never felt the call of God. After leaving school, I went straight to work in order to assist my mum, who by this time had six other children to feed. I dabbled with two or three jobs, varying from being a clerk, to working on a building site, and finally being a policeman.

I remember having a 'soft' heart, talking to minor offenders rather than arresting them, and not feeling within me the toughness for the job as needed. Unknowingly, I was being moulded for a different calling. I quit my job at the

Manatita as an 18-yr old policeman in Grenada, W.I.

age of twenty-one, took the opportunity that nursing offered me, and travelled to England in search of exploration and a different life. I spent two weeks with my youngest and loving aunt, and then started my vocation as a nurse at Hillingdon Hospital, Uxbridge, Middlesex.

*****

It is September 1982; I am sitting at home in a two-bedroom maisonette. Things are different now. I am a responsible father and husband in London, England. I have a very beautiful, devoted, and dutiful wife, and a two-year old son. Today is my day off work. I am sitting downstairs when I hear a loud sound coming from the direction of the hallway. I go expectantly to the doorway. A rather large packet drops to the floor. It is addressed to me. I open it and see a book inside. *"The Path: Autobiography of a Western Yogi,"* by *Swami Kriyananda.* I begin to read and a very powerful thrill runs through my Heart. I have come home.

One week later, I am again influenced by two books: *"The Bhagavad Gita, As It Is"* by His Divine Grace, A.C. Bhaktivedanta, Swami Prabupada, and, *"Meditation: Paths to Tranquillity,"* by Peter Russell. Taking an address and telephone number from the latter, within a week I had found the Sri Chinmoy Centre, became inspired immediately by the writings and personality of Sri Chinmoy, and accepted him as my Guru. As regards the Centre, since that very first day, October 1st, 1982, I have never stopped going.

November 2nd 2006

CHAPTER TWO

Spiritual Transitioning

"Transformation of the body shows us how pure we can be. Liberation of the vital shows us how dynamic we can be. Revelation of the mind shows us how vast we can be. Manifestation of the heart shows us how divine we can be."

-*Sri Chinmoy.*
Fifty Freedom-Boats To One Golden Shore, Part 4, (1974), Agni Press.

Spiritual Transitioning, as it is meant in this context, is rather like moving from the old into the new; from unconscious awareness to conscious Truth, from a labyrinth or chasm into a realm brimming with effulgent Light. It begins with spiritual awakening. Speaking of this re-birthing to Nicodemus, The Christ said:

"That which is born of the flesh is flesh and that which is born of the Spirit is spirit"

The Holy Bible: King James Version. John 3:6.

In my case, it was quite sudden, unravelling itself with joy and intensity, while reading *The Path,* as mentioned in the first Chapter. It is as if one moment I was enmeshed in the concepts of heaven, fiery hell and eternal damnation as punishment for sins, and in the next, awakened to the doctrine of re-incarnation, karma, Self-discovery, and the immortality of the Soul:

"Weapons cannot cleave the soul. Fire cannot burn the soul. Water cannot drench the soul. Wind cannot dry the Soul." *The Son, Scene 2, (1973),* Agni Press. *(*Originally from the Gita, Hindu scriptures)

One must remember that I came from a Christian (Anglican) background, had no outside help in making this major transition, nor any prior knowledge of Swami Kriyananda's philosophy on Karma and Re-incarnation, and yet immediately accepted them, and even incorporated this knowledge into daily life. Here I was experiencing a change, brought about not by my Anglican beliefs of heaven, hell and punishment or rewards. Rather it was more like a directive from my Soul, into the reality of eternal life in which human souls participate by reincarnating along millennia, until finally returning to their Eternal Home. I found this new and mystical approach, very refreshing and incredibly real.

No more would I fear a Man (God), with long flowing beard, in a geographical place somewhere in the sky, or the possibility of burning in everlasting fire if I continued to do wrong. Instead, I now began to see a loving and compassionate God, felt an intensity of faith in the unconquerable nature of the Soul, and indeed saw myself as not only being made in the image of God, but as God Itself (Spirit). Knowing that I am the immortal Soul, was never born and would never die, gave me new hope and the illumination to see the future with vision, trust, clarity and promise. This all took place in the depth of my Being.

At this point, and for the benefit of my Christian readers, I wish to say that the spiritual life as explained by Yoga philosophy, encapsulated my beliefs. It also cemented my faith in Christian values with which I was brought up from early childhood, and of which even to this day, I am quite proud.

Of course Spiritual Transitioning would be incomplete without practical changes, some done consciously, and others simply appearing even before one becomes conscious of them. I guess that the Supreme, and the Soul in its wisdom, were now taking care of everything needed, as long as that inner yearning, earnestness or longing remained for a more fruitful and fulfilling life. For my part, I soon began to avoid unwholesome friends, parties, drinking and so forth, and became a vegetarian. This helped me to facilitate an easier transition into the meditative life, as well as becoming closer to God.

I acknowledge that we are all different, and some would approach day to day transitioning in other ways. In my case, I was really only a light social drinker. I did not smoke, nor used hard or non-medicinal drugs, and was moving towards a vegetarian lifestyle anyway. So the things recommended by my Guru were pretty easy for me to follow. Of course one cannot stop friends laughing or thinking one strange. They will also at first encourage you to go to parties and later resent you for not going. At home you may have difficulty when trying to set up a Shrine (a place for spiritual practices) in your home.

Here again I was fortunate. I was married at the time, had a separate room which I used, and while my loved one may have found this sudden change unusual, she remained a tolerant and caring wife.

The biggest challenge for me was with making the transition from a life of lower vital pleasure (the sex life), to a life of self-control. Interestingly enough, as if getting help from an unseen source, my first few years were pure and very devotional. They also included some loving spiritual experiences which enhanced my ability to be more self- giving and caring in my daily tasks. This is another aspect of transitioning in a positive way.

One begins to look at life and the world differently, to be kinder, nobler, more self- sacrificing and so forth. I began to look at my body as a Temple or Instrument for a Higher Purpose, and as such tried to keep it healthy and sacred. This inevitably included exercise, diet, and other life-style changes. My Guru recommended them all in his writings.

Again, the time came when an acquired discipline, led to a spontaneous inner urge to rise early in the morning to pray and meditate, and to try to carry its naturally joyful outcome to my usual environment. This happened at home, on the streets, on the buses, trains and at work with my fellow colleagues. Pretty soon, people around me started seeing differences in my behaviour and began commenting about it. Even my parents did the same. Were they into it? Never! My mother did not understand, and my father used to laugh at me. Still, the time came – many years later - when my mother appreciated me with reverence, and my father just couldn't be bothered to tease me anymore. This striving for obedience to a Higher Cause I continue to practice diligently, even to this very moment

My mother died on August 9th 2011. She knew her time had come and asked for the priest and her children to be called from various countries, two days before she died. Alas! I did not make it in time, but down in Grenada, where she died, I was able to sing some illumining songs, partake in prayers and officiate at her beautiful funeral ceremony. Of course I had spoken to mom on her 77th birthday just before, and so I was reassured both from without and within that all would be well. This was heart-warming. It was also a joy to be with my brothers and sisters all in one place, after a very long time.

I alluded to the difficulty with transcending the 'lower Vital', a little earlier in this Chapter. Something that Sri Chinmoy taught was crucial and imperative for the higher meditative experiences. The time came when I experienced difficulties which I won't dwell on, but it is useful from the standpoint that my Guru taught that, until one realise God, one has to be constantly vigilante and is never 'safe'. Unwanted experiences, while they may set us back somewhat, do have their roles in helping us to be watchful, cautious

… to not take things for granted. Still, I did have an experience which affected my spiritual focus for a short while. Am I safe now? Certainly not! But today, I am even more prudent, discriminating and more watchful than I have ever been.

There are other ways of transitioning for the disciple as he/she tries to manifest his/her Guru's teachings. Through spiritual discipline, many find that they can bring forward their hidden potential in areas such as music and the arts, sports – a favourite of Sri Chinmoy – and in Self-transcendence, going beyond their limits in swimming, cycling, mountaineering and other feats of endeavour. Of course the Sri Chinmoy Centre manifests or serves the public in many ways, whether it's through drama, holding races, Sri Chinmoy Oneness-Home Peace Runs/World Harmony Runs, school and humanitarian activities, as well as many other aspects of the Master's teaching. Someone will write all about these things one day, and I have also covered this a little in Chapter fourteen.

I wish, however, to state that one undergoes a kind of change in one's angle of vision. With the encouragement and guidance of the Master, one begins to see things in a new light and suddenly so much more appears within the realm of possibility. So in my case, I began to run more, swim more and so forth. Although I was able to swim, it took me three months just to learn the front crawl. A further three years of training and I was ready to attempt the English Channel. A feat prior to meeting Sri Chinmoy, I would not even have conceived of. I did not swim in the end as I had problems with the cold weather, but many of my friends not only attempted, but were also successful in this gigantic challenge.

I also took up running in earnest, and ran many marathons, 47 mile races and even 100K. I race-walked for 12 hours a few times with very encouraging results, my best being 50 miles in 12-hrs. One can read about Sri Chinmoy's philosophy on sport and physical fitness in *The Outer Running and The Inner Running,* but I have dedicated Chapter seven of this book to the spirit of Self-Transcendence. Let's just say that the aim of life is progress, not success or failure, but to go beyond, beyond, into the ever- transcending beyond; to remove all limitations, all that is bothering us and standing in our way. This is the message that I understood from this remarkable human being, who was himself, as ever, a perfect example of his teachings.

Finally, Spiritual Transitioning can present challenges on a more subtle level. Sri Chinmoy teaches that Light must descend into darkness, for only then can it transform and illumine darkness. This is what the Avatar (Divine

Incarnation) does. However, on a more microcosmic level, the seeker faces this transformation brought about by the Higher Light on a daily basis. The aspirant's prayer and meditative life enters at a deeper level, into his insecurities, fears, jealousies, ego … and so forth, in order to bring them to the fore for illumination. This process can be quite painful.

One of the fastest ways for transcending negativities is through working together in a spiritual community, by soulful self-giving together on various projects, and of course also out there in the big wide world. Still, it is rewarding in the sense that one finds oneself becoming more tolerant, more acutely aware of others burdens, and as the Light permeates even further, one is generally happier to serve and offer kind words and deeds to one's fellow beings. I need

Sri Chinmoy in Auckland, New Zealand, 1989

not mention that of course the Master's guidance is always there.

I hope that I have given the reader an insight into the power of transformation through Faith, Meditation and Prayer, for that is what it really is. My perception is that no Spiritual Transitioning can take place without the Will or Inner Dictates of the Supreme. One is always reliant upon Divine Grace, but with an ardent, devout, disciplined and surrendered life to the Supreme; with inner receptivity and outer capacity, Sri Chinmoy teaches that everything can be accomplished.

- Manatita, December 12th, 2011.

CHAPTER THREE

Spiritual Experiences

"Life is lovely therefore I live, prayer is lovely therefore I pray,
Creation is lovely therefore I love"

-*Sri Chinmoy.*
Te*n Thousand Flower-Flames, Part 1,* (1979). Agni Press,

It was about 19.55hrs that evening when He inwardly came .... Strong, forceful, powerful .... He was as sudden and unexpected as a butterfly at night. Vaguely aware of a most beautiful stage at the Royal Albert Hall, London, I was sitting absorbed in the shimmering rays of its electronic effects: red, blue, green, yellow .... A myriad of dazzlingly colourful spectrums of light shone before me as the Grace of Guru flooded my being with His love, sweetness and delight.

I guess that I was being subconsciously prepared for this experience that day, and that what happened was the result of a culmination of imbibed inspirations at the Royal Albert Hall. That afternoon, May 19th, 2008, I had gone somewhat early to the venue. Here I was enchanted by the magnificent complexity of the Royal Albert Hall, its stunning red drapes, majesty and visual beauty. On stage, Boris Purushottama Grebenshikov – a Russian musician and composer - and his band were practising, surrounded by a gigantic arrangement of flowers and plants. Fresh, fragrant and colourful, they embodied a natural spontaneity, purity and bloom, as they blended easily into the setting of the Hall.

On stage also, and to the right, was a 10x8 foot polystyrene cutting of Ganesha – the elephant god of Protection - , and another of Saraswati, consort of Brahma, the Hindu god of creation, playing her Veena. Saraswati is known as the goddess of learning, the arts, music and the Saraswati River. They both looked stunningly alive, adding all the more to the beauty and ambience of an incredibly wonderful setting, a job well done.

All those things inspired me, together with the constant droves of people who entered steadily through the different doors as the evening gathered pace.

Previously Sri Chinmoy had told Boris Purushottama Grebenshikov that he would see him at the Royal Albert Hall, and I was perhaps beginning to feel His presence in the large and eager audience assembled here.

So here I was, sitting up front, and not more than twenty-four feet from the stage ... the experience of beauty and peace from within was gradually taking hold. High up above me, I was vaguely aware of some sort of preliminary programme being shown prior to the performance, and of the disciple who was sitting next to me at that time.

Here I sat, gradually drifting further into the experience. My inner being was flooded with peace, tranquillity and love so forcefully, that it was quite some time before I regained sufficient focus to enjoy the performance.

What is a spiritual experience? Perhaps the reader will have some ideas. Here, however, I will attempt to recount my own. Sometime in the fall of 1982, I was sitting in front of my shrine at home, looking intently at the transcendental picture of Sri Chinmoy. Suddenly a non-familiar state came over me, and I seemed to lose control of what I was doing. This was accompanied by a subtle fear, thus causing the experience to dissipate.

Knowing by faith that this was something associated with my meditation, I spoke to Bhavani – at that time a prominent member of the London Sri Chinmoy Centre – about it. I recall that she told me not to be afraid, to open up myself to the experience and to surrender to the Supreme[1]. Indeed this was all I needed at the time, and from then on I had no problems with the experiences that came along the way.

Spiritual experiences can take many shapes and forms. I have known devotees to speak of shaking, crying, laughing, or having a feeling of peace, seeing visions, hearing a sound and much more. I have personally experienced intense love for humanity, tears, and a forceful energy which affected my posture and breathing, and thrills running in and through my being. Some of my religious friends have spoken of 'speaking in tongues' and also shouting out the name of the Lord.

As a beginner-seeker, I wish to write with Zen mind, beginner's mind. Nevertheless, I would say that for me a spiritual experience has never been painful, fearful or sensational. It has always made me feel closer to God, and came with a purity which pushed me in the direction of service and surrender – a deeper yearning to serve God in mankind and to surrender to His will.

It is with this in mind that I would strongly suggest to anyone who may feel any fear, pain or emotionalism, to approach their Mentors for guidance, especially where there is a need for clarity on the inner workings of the psyche.

Spiritual experiences have come to me quite suddenly. Sometimes I have had a foretaste, but mostly I did not know nor could I predict. It seemed that I would do everything right and not feel anything great at all. While at other times, with everything seemingly going wrong, I would still get great spiritual experiences. My perception of Sri Chinmoy's philosophy is that everything would come naturally and should not be forced. He also emphasised purity in the Vital (see Chapter's six and thirteen), and the importance of being ready for the experience. This is important in minimising the risks of things going wrong.

One day in late 1982, I was meditating at my shrine, when I suddenly felt a powerful surge of energy. A very strong 'Force' was flowing in and through me. The thought suddenly came to my head that I should try out this newly acquired power. I subsequently stretched out my hand to my lighted candle, and commanded it to blow out. At that point I felt a great strain on my forehead, the power immediately left me, and yes, I never tried this fruitless exercise ever again. I am afraid I still have some work to do as far as the need for purity and the transformation of the ego.

Spiritual experiences, as I perceive them, seem to come from God's goodness or God's will (Grace). It is a gift of the Supreme. One day in the early 1980's, I was sitting at a conference called 'The Italian Experience', and listening to some prominent speakers talking about some aspects of my profession. Suddenly, I felt myself being lifted up and taken to a place of deep calm, peace and comfort. I soon found it a struggle to hold on to the lecture, and subsequently lost all memory of what was being said. Indeed, perhaps it was fortunate for me that I was sitting at the back and so did not attract attention.

Writing in the Bible, the Apostle Paul says: - "For by grace are you saved through faith, and not of yourselves, it is a gift of God and not of works, lest any man should boast." *The Holy Bible: King James Version.* Ephesians 2: V.8, 9.

This is how I have come to feel about spiritual experiences.

I have felt deep inner thrills through listening attentively to my Master, by hearing him talk, sing and meditate, by telephone, reading his writings and in many other significant ways. I will relate one more experience here. One day, I attended an event in Manhattan, probably in the early nineties. It was at a function in honour of Sri Chinmoy. I was sitting at a table at the back with a few disciples from New York.

Once again a great wave of peace overpowered me, as if it was coming directly from the Master sitting up front. Being conscious of the disciples around me, I somehow managed to pull myself away, and sat down in the semi-lotus posture, in the hallway of that particular floor of the Hotel. Here waves of peace kept flowing in and through me periodically. It was as if I would be granted a brief respite intermittently, followed by a continuation of the experience. This lasted for some time. Much later, when I came to, I felt quite cold. In the nearby hallway, I could see a very familiar girl disciple smiling at me lovingly. I returned the smile, got up and returned to the function.

I have had experiences that have taken other forms. While not necessarily inner encounters as such, they are part of life experiences that come along the way. There have been intuitive flashes which protected the writer from arguments, and helped also to avoid more serious problems. Again, the intense identification with others ills, has at times brought great pain. There is also the additional inner 'suffering' meted out when one does 'wrong', and also the feeling that another of God's children has been hurt, even if unintentionally, can sometimes lead to great inner sorrow.

According to my understanding of Sri Chinmoy's writings, spiritual experiences may or may not come, and are not a necessary or indispensable indicator in the seeker's development. While they may come because the Supreme gives them to us, the focus should still remain on love of God, and in striving to do the Will of the Supreme. Nevertheless, spiritual experiences can be significant pointers on the way, and indeed may be very useful in serving the divinity in God and man.

Sri Chinmoy has written extensively, and has described – as one speaking with authority – some of the more exalted spiritual experiences. One can read about this higher knowledge in *Samadhi and Siddhi, the Summit of God-life*, or *Light of the Beyond: Teachings of an Illumined Master*.

He has also discussed certain topics in conversations with his disciples. One particular experience that inspired me came from the book *Beyond Within*, written by Sri Chinmoy, *and i*n a passage entitled *Joy in Surrender*. Here Sri Chinmoy writes lovingly of the constant joy that comes with surrender to God's will, to the extent that one sees and feels this joy in the trees, cars and everything that one touches. (*Beyond Within: Philosophy for the Inner Life, P441, (1985)*, Agni Press).

Perhaps it behoves us all to seek these higher experiences of God through living an unconditionally surrendered life to the Supreme.

-Monday 29th December, 2008.
Deway Asajaya Room, Grand Margherita Hotel, Kuching, Malaysia.

CHAPTER FOUR

A Glimpse Into
The Early Life of Sri Chinmoy

"Make your whole life a garland of beauty, a garland of purity,
A garland of joy and a garland of luminosity,
And place it at the Feet of your Lord Beloved Supreme"

-Sri Chinmoy
Seventy-Seven Thousand Service-Trees, Part 16, No. 15,555 (1999), Agni Press.

So who was Sri Chinmoy? What shaped him and prepared him for the work that he was to do in the West? Was he influenced by anything or anyone? Have a look at this poem below:

I Have Inherited

"My sister Lily's love and determination I have inherited.

My sister Arpita's concern and service I have inherited.

My brother Chita's poetry and sacrifice I have inherited.

My brother Hriday's philosophy and wisdom I have inherited.

My brother Mantu's patience and detachment I have inherited.

My sister Ahana's music and immensity I have inherited.

My Mother Yoga Maya's psychic tears and surrender I have inherited.

My Father Shashi Kumar's inner confidence and outer triumph I have inherited."

To the Streaming Tears of My Mother's Heart and to the Brimming Smiles of My Mother's Soul. P. 1 (1994). Agni Press.

Early Life in India

Sri· Chinmoy's parents: Shashi Kumar and Yogamaya Ghose

Sir Chinmoy was born in Chittagong, in the village of Shakpura, East Bengal, (now Bangladesh) India, on August 27th, 1931. He was the last of seven children, being preceded by three elder brothers and three sisters. Sri Chinmoy tells us that his early life was full of mischief and adventure; he was also naughty and very restless. He used to pinch his elder brothers and sisters, but this was matched by the unshakable and dedicated love which rained down on him from his Mother, Yoga Maya Ghose. This same love was shown to him by his Father, Shashi Kumar Ghose and his entire family.

Before Sri Chinmoy was born, his brother Chitta had a number of dreams that his Mother would give birth to a great Soul. She was a great devotee of Sri Krishna, and so she felt that perhaps he was sending his dearest devotee into their simple, humble and prayerful family. Chitta, however, felt that our Guruji would be a spiritual Soul of the highest magnitude. *(Ibid. p 5)*.

Of course Sri Chinmoy's Mother, as mentioned before, was a great bhakta of Sri Krishna. Sri Chinmoy said of her cooking, that it was sitting in the temple for hours and hours praying and meditating. She prayed to Sri Krishna, that like his Mother Devaki, she, Guruji's mother, could also have a special child. We learn of her great devotion from the Master who said that her faith was always in her worship, in God, never in doctors. This not only allowed her to show him concern and affection, but to pray to God to save his life from smallpox and other dangers, while on his adventurous jaunts. *(Ibid. pp 16-19)*.

There is a story told by Sri Chinmoy that once his Mother attended a performance based on a play of the life of Sri Chaitanya, the great Bengali Spiritual Master. Sri Chinmoy takes up the story:

"At one point in the story, Sri Chaitanya's Mother was shedding tears because her son had taken a solemn vow to renounce the world and follow the spiritual life. My own Mother in the audience became racked with sobs.

My brother Chitta attempted to console her: "Mother, don't cry! Sri Chaitanya was disobedient to his Mother but we will never be so. We will remain with you always. Have no fear."

My Mother protested. "But you do not understand why I am crying. It is because I want all my children, sons and daughters alike, to follow that Path. I long for each one of them to be able to realise God in this life!" Such was my Mother's inner cry," *(Ibid. p 23)*.

Sri Chinmoy was born in his village home in the month of August, (Bhadra, in Bengali), and so his Mother composed a couplet in Bengali thus:

Ek bhada jar

Sonar madal tar

It says that he who is born in the month of Bhadra is definitely going to beat the golden kettledrum. The golden kettledrum is being played in the Heavens by the cosmic Gods. Sri Chinmoy was given the nickname Madal, which means "kettledrum." Of this he says:

"Perhaps it was because I was always making so much noise!" Sometimes my grandmother would find my liveliness too much for her, and she would say, "This kettledrum will bring about total destruction of the family!" *(Ibid. p 7)*.

His mother, however, felt that it would bring him abundant name and fame. That he was destined to be played on by the gods and goddesses in the skies. Sri Chinmoy's first name, his horoscopic name, however, was Ganapati - the elephant god. Ganapati is the giver of realisation and also the scribe who noted down the Mahabharata from the Sage Vyasa in one sitting. *(My Brother Chitta, Page 60, (1998), Agni Press)*.

His real name, Chinmoy, means 'full of divine consciousness', and was given to him by his brother Chitta, who described it thus:

"In 1936, when we visited the Sri Aurobindo Ashram, the Ashram Secretary, Nolini Kanta Gupta, wanted to know Madal's real name, because Madal is a nickname. I was a little bit puzzled. What suitable name could we give to our youngest brother? Our eldest brother's name is Hriday Ranjan. My name is Chitta Ranjan. My younger brother's name is Manoranjan. Then Prana Ranjan was coming to my mind to give as Madal's real name, but it was not satisfying my heart. All on a sudden, I got an inner message. A divine voice echoed and re-echoed in my heart: "Chinmoy, Chinmoy!" My human mind never thought that this name would one day be accepted, loved and adored by countless truth-seekers and God-lovers." *(Ibid. p 59)*

Sri Chinmoy himself teaches us that he had many names:

"I had so many names in the Ashram! My dearest friend, who saw something in me long before anybody else, used to call me Chinny. Someone else used to call me Chinnymoyda. 'Chinny' means sugar and 'moyda' means flour. When I was very young, some people used to call me a name that meant 'Japanese doll' because they felt that I was cute. Then some people, especially girls, gave me a name meaning 'fire' because my eyes were always red, wide open and very fiery; they felt there was no compassion in my eyes. Others called me Jogisamrat, Jogibar or Jogiraj." *Sri Chinmoy Answers, Part 8, (1997)*, Agni Press.

As a little boy he knew lots of stories from the Hindu epic, the *Mahabharata*, taught to him by his Mother. It was her way of trying to get him to fall asleep in the afternoon, so as to avoid his going out into the blazing sun. He was deceptive, though, and would sometimes play tricks on her, pretending that he was fast asleep. When she herself went to sleep, he would go with the servant to pluck fruits and eat them. His mother would always forgive his deception, because she was always conquered by his smile. This unparalleled smile he carried with him to the West to the joy of all his disciples.

It is worth noting here that Guruji told us many tales and wrote many stories and plays, as well as writing numerous other books much later while in the West. Perhaps some may have been influenced by the regular readings from his Mother and his listening to her tales from the great Indian epics.

Guru's sister Arpita used to teach him the letters of the English alphabet when he was about four years old, as she saw that he had no interest in learning the letters of the Bengali alphabet. Writing of this, Sri Chinmoy said that God gave his sister divine insight. He did not go to school very often, but used to roam for the whole day in town, or go to the Karnaphuli River to see the boats and ships. He was taught by his brother and tutor, and he must have showed promise even then, as when exams came, he always stood first. Even so, he would always cry when he had to return home from town, as in his own words: 'studying was too much, too much.' *My Father Shashi Kumar Ghose: Affection-Life Compassion-Heart Illumination-Mind, Page 5, (1992)*, Agni Press.

When Sri Chinmoy's Mother was dying, she encouraged Chitta to stay with her rather than go to the Ashram (spiritual hermitage), while she was alive. She thought that he would feel sad if she died in his absence. However, when the time came for him to go, she encouraged him to buy a new ticket and to go to the Ashram. Such was her devotion to the spiritual life. She died of goitre, a big tumour on the left side of her neck. She was not quite 50, and died just one year after Madal's Father, who was 62 years old, when he passed away. They had a deep soul's connection, and, according to Sri Chinmoy, were related to him in his past incarnations.

Prior to his Mother's death, family members read out the *Gita* – a sacred book from the Hindu scripture – constantly during her last few days. She wanted to make sure that she prepared herself. Before she died, she called for Madal, (Guruji) and placed his hand in his eldest brother's hand, telling him to take responsibility for Madal's life. She then gave her Madal a smile, and in a few seconds passed away. It was at the beginning of the year 1944.

A few months later, Sri Chinmoy went to live permanently in the Sri Aurobindo Ashram. We know also that all his brothers and sisters went to live there. In fact he was the last to do so at 12, although he initially visited a few times. (*To The Streaming Tears Of My Mother's Heart And To The Brimming Smiles Of My Mother's Soul. P. 26; 35; 38. (1994).* Agni Press.)

Sri Chinmoy has told us that both his parents were extremely spiritual. His Father was a kind man who worked as a railway officer of the Assam-Bengal railway. He worked his way up to become Head Inspector of the whole line. Sri Chinmoy used to enjoy riding on the train so much! (Today there are

A Youthful Sri Chinmoy

Peace Trains named after him in the West). Guru's Father also became the owner and manager of a bank. The name of the bank was Griha-Lakshmi, which means "House of Lakshmi" He used to say that he was extremely happy with a son who brought such life, vitality and enthusiasm into the family. *My Brother Chitta, Page 12, 63. (1998),* Agni Press.

Right from his childhood, young Madal (Sri Chinmoy) had tremendous eagerness for learning. He was always inquisitive and asking questions. His grandmother felt that he was going to be a great writer like Ganapati, and his Mother used to say: "When you grow up, you will know everything, you will have all the answers."

He had a desire to write and print books and in 1946, at age 14, he rendered Sri Aurobindo's story, *'Kshamar Adarsha'*, *'The Ideal of Forgiveness'*, into Bengali verse. Sri Aurobindo – the Spiritual Master at the Ashram at that time – said: "It is a fine piece of poetry. He has capacity. Tell him to continue." *(Ibid. pp 60-61).*

Guru did not continue studying in school, but studied on his own at the library for hours. He also had mentors as well as being helped by the Ashrams secretary, Nolini Kanta Gupta. This assisted in cultivating his English literature capacity. He was taught English metre by a young man called Romen whom he met on the street, and he was able to write his first poem in English called *The Golden Flute*, which earned him 25 rupees. *The Absolute,* a lofty and poetic masterpiece which almost every disciple knows by heart, was Sri Chinmoy's third poem. *(Ibid. p 65).*

As indicated previously, Sri Chinmoy travelled to Pondicherry, South India, where he took up residence at the Sri Aurobindo Ashram. Sri Aurobindo was a scholar and poet, who studied in England. Upon his return to India, he had initially taken up the cause of fighting for India's freedom. Soon, however, he turned to spirituality through many lofty visions given to him by great sages of the past. Sri Aurobindo was recognised as a great Spiritual Master and God-realised Soul. He was the founder of a spiritual community, and it was there that our Guruji and his family took residence for spiritual practices.

Sri Chinmoy began to explore more the journey of the inner life while taking part in other activities at the Ashram. Sri Chinmoy's unceasing yearning for God was soon filled with profound experiences of the highest bliss infinite. He meditated constantly, sometimes up to 14 hours a day or more, remaining in

A Young Sri Chinmoy, 1964

deep contemplation for hours on end. In addition to this, and in keeping with the Ashram's practice of Integral Yoga, Guruji also immersed himself in sports, and other social activities at the Ashram. There he excelled in a number of activities including sprinting and poetry.

This was perhaps a forerunner to his sportive talent and flair for

organising Marathon races, Masters Games and other sporting activities with his disciples internationally, much later on. He was also to lay emphasis on the physical, and the Integral Yoga of the Sri Aurobindo Ashram. In this our Master utilised and added many more ideas, effectively making it his own path to progress.

Still, Sri Chinmoy's yearning for a greater vision continued, and in time he saw his true purpose of a higher realisation and manifestation unfold. The Master speaks of a most exalted experience while meditating one day, in

Sri Chinmoy as a young sprinter- athlete in the Ashram

which the Supreme came to him and revealed to him His 'inner command' for Sri Chinmoy to travel to the West to serve

seekers there. Sri Chinmoy expresses this in a most elevating and profound way, which leaves the reader in no doubt that the Master is communicating from direct experience:

"Whenever I had the opportunity, I flew to the edge of the ever-blue sea and took my seat there in solitude. My bird of consciousness, dancing slowly, rose to the sky and lost itself up there.

On that occasion - it was a full moon night – as I gazed and gazed upon the blue-white horizon, I found only a sea of sweet and serene light. All was engulfed,

Sri Chinmoy in Samadhi

as it were, in an infinite Ocean of Light which played lovingly on the sweet ripples.

My finite consciousness was in quest of the infinite and immortal. I drank deeply of ambrosia, and was floating on an illumined ocean. It seemed that I no longer existed on this earth."

Sri Chinmoy goes on to tell us that without knowing why, something put an end to his sweet dream. His thoughts became depressed and he felt that everything was "useless". He began to ask himself why he should not leave this mortal world for his eternal abode in heaven. He continues:

"A sudden flash of lightning appeared over my head. Looking up with awe and bewilderment, I found above me my Beloved, the King of the Universe, looking at me, His radiant Face overcast with sorrow.

"Father," I asked, approaching Him, "what makes Thy Face so sad?"

"How can I be happy, my son, if you do not wish to be my companion, and help Me in My Mission? I have, concealed in the world, millions of sweet plans which I shall unravel. If My children do not help Me in My play, how can I have My divine Manifestation here on earth?"

Profoundly moved, I bowed and promised. "Father, I will be Thy faithful companion, loving and sincere, throughout Eternity. Shape me and make me  worthy of my part in Thy cosmic play and Thy divine Mission." *Eternity's Breath: Aphorisms and Essays, Page 81, (1975),* Agni Press.

Following this inner command, and ably assisted by some close friends, Sri Chinmoy travelled to the West where he arrived on the 13th April, 1964, after spending some 20 years in the Ashram.

In 1964, while in New York City, USA, the Master spent a brief period working at the Indian Consulate. However, he soon gathered western seekers who were charmed by his vision and spiritual wisdom. They invited him to speak of this philosophical

Sri Chinmoy, 1972

wisdom, and not long after the foundations of his Path were soon established, initially in Puerto Rico.

Quite soon Sri Chinmoy Centres developed in the United States and elsewhere and increased worldwide to include all continents and many countries. Sri Chinmoy himself became revered and loved by many students, luminaries, dignitaries, Heads of State, sportsmen and women from around the Globe. These include Olympic hero Jesse Owens, Pope Paul VI, Mohammed Ali, Maestros Pablo Casals and Leonard Bernstein. He was also fond of the Olympic gold medallist Sudahota Carl Lewis, former President Gorbachev, Nelson Mandela, Mother Theresa and many others.

Sri Chinmoy with Nelson Mandela and Mayor Dinkins, New York

Finally, it is worth mentioning, that Sri Chinmoy had mutual friendships and mentorships with great individuals, in great institutions. One such institution or world body is the United Nations. (See Chapter 14, Part 2) Sri Chinmoy showed great admiration and respect for the third United Nations Secretary- General and great servant of peace, U Thant. He was also fond of Dag-Hammarskjold, the second Secretary-General, and spoke of Dag Hammarskjold's 'mind brilliance' and 'heart's oneness', in a tribute to the UN Secretary-General, on his birth anniversary, July 291 1976.Throughout his life, Sri Chinmoy identified with the higher ideals of the United Nations of peace, love, harmony and universal oneness.

- Manatita 3rd Feb, 2012.

CHAPTER FIVE

A Glimpse into the Personality of Sri Chinmoy

"When peace is multiplied, Truth is multiplied.
When Truth is multiplied, Love is multiplied.
When Love is multiplied, God is multiplied"

- Sri Chinmoy
God's Hour, (1973), Agni Press.

Sri Chinmoy was a man absorbed in God. As such he was universal. Indeed everything He did or said exemplified this universality, impartiality and love for all beings here on Earth and in the worlds beyond. The writer saw him as one of God's Son's and an Advocate in the era in which he lived. He also demonstrated a unique kind of love. In an attempt to give the reader a glimpse of Sri Chinmoy, the writer will express this chapter in a way which may seem partial. It is important, however, to remember that he saw Sri Chinmoy as a Being who represented Something Higher …, a universal God-lover who cared for all and loved all life and served as such for the evolution of ALL Mankind.

I remember Sri Chinmoy as being prayerful, cheerful, joyful and loving, as well as having many other uniquely positive virtues. That sweet simplicity, loving gaze, sunlit serenity

Offering a blessingful flower

and inner peace always enwrapped him and made an indelible impression of him on others as a man steeped in God. In his presence, one felt a powerful manifestation of a tremendous sense of inner beauty, dispassion and childlike sweetness.

Sri Chinmoy also showed outward munificence and charm, accompanied by an inner stillness, which was to remain with him all his life. Of course, he

was an incredibly dynamic person, a quality that showed and manifested in his numerous activities and physical prowess around the globe. This was to be expected, as he was a supreme athlete in his early youth, and the decathlon champion at the Sri Aurobindo Ashram, Pondicherry, for many years.

Guru enjoyed playing tennis, a sport in which He participated quite frequently with many of his disciples, admirers, luminaries and political friends, as well as Olympians and other athletes around the world. At such times he would laugh much, and enjoyed sending his opponents all around the Court, as he burst with laughter. He was so childlike in his ways, and had a mischievous and fun-filled grin which was a joy to behold. Incredibly disciplined, Guru would pay great attention to the game, scoring out the number of games quite accurately, and inspiring his player-friends to do their best.

I remember him playing with Sudahota Carl Lewis, Narada Michael Walden, and

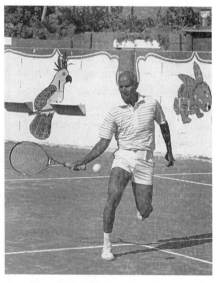

Enjoying a game of tennis

tennis greats such as Steffi Graf and Ilie Nastase. For me it seemed significant, indeed a part of His life's work, that Guru enjoyed meeting with dignitaries, world leaders, Popes and political leaders. It helped him to inspire them, to show an exemplary life and to convey his message of universal Oneness, and love for God. This he was to continue to do all his life, and he found innovative and original ways of honouring them through constantly self-giving methods and ideas.

One such idea was the Lifting up the World with a Oneness Heart programme, in which a specially designed apparatus was used to literally lift others overhead, as a way of honouring their contribution to society.

Mohammed Ali, Carl Lewis and Nelson Mandela were lifted through this programme. Of particular note here was Sri Chinmoy's love for Nelson Mandela. He was also full of admiration for world figures such as President Gorbachev, and Mother Theresa. Perhaps it was a way of expressing fatherly gratitude, for these were human beings who had worked tirelessly, for the good and upliftment of all mankind. Guru also felt that they exemplified courage, determination

Lifting Up The World With A Oneness-Heart programme

and selflessness by their noble sacrifices.

Much later Guruji would go on to lift phenomenal weights and other heavy objects such as planes, elephants, cars and people in varying acrobatic formations using specially built apparatuses for the occasion. Many of his feats were recorded and seen on TV. He never ceased to amaze.

Mother Theresa and the Sisters of Charity. She is holding the Sri Chinmoy Oneness- Home Peace Torch

Sri Chinmoy weightlifting an unprecedented 7063¾, 1986.

Well into His sixties, Guru was still a tremendous athlete and a great motivator and inspirer. Sri Chinmoy would often compose songs for his many guests, and would chat and laugh with them considerably. He had a way of bringing out the best in others by constantly highlighting their good qualities and in some unexplained manner, frequently bringing it to the fore. He gave his friends lots of presents, made them feel at ease, and they would occasionally have a tour of the beautiful Pilgrim- Museum, a small house at Aspiration-Ground, dedicated to Sri Chinmoy's art. This would sometimes be preceded or followed by a vegetarian meal at the Annam Brahma restaurant, some 100 metres from the Aspiration-Temple grounds.

Sri Chinmoy loved sports. Whether it was weightlifting, running, swimming or mountain-climbing, He would encourage His disciples to participate. Indeed there were many annual and celebratory events, including ultra-distance runs such as the 47 mile race, which was held on his birthday, and the 12 hr. walk, celebrating April 13th, the day that Sri Chinmoy arrived in the West. Many of Guru's disciples, inspired by his emphasis

Parade around Jamaica, Queens. African Centre's float.

on exercise, completed incredible feats such as swimming the English Channel, or completing races from 24 hrs. to 3100 miles!! Assisted by Alo Devi, Sri Chinmoy also supervised events such as Jala Ramani – a swimming fun-filled competition that disciples did - Sports Day, Madal Bal Circus and our annual Parade in Jamaica, Queens, New York. This was a real energy-booster for the disciples and residents there, who looked forward to this joyful pageantry of marchers and floats, with great anticipation.

Other forms of sport that Sri Chinmoy enjoyed included basketball, push-ups and sit- ups, as well as working out on his many and varied machines built with his guidance by some of his disciples. This he did frequently in the early hours of the morning. Sri Chinmoy sometimes shot baskets with us at Madal Circus, a one day event he created for us to have innocent fun. How Guru loved this game! He would usually play for about half an hour, even with a bad back and painful legs. We, his disciples, enjoyed watching very much and supported and encouraged him joyfully. On Sports Day he would sometimes race with the disciples. He also competed in the World Masters Games.

Sri Chinmoy, 1993 at a UN function for Martin Luther King

Standing about 5ft 8 ins tall and weighing just over 140 pounds, this simple, balding yet handsome man was essentially slim in his youth but gained weight and bulk over the years. This was probably due to a knee injury which he sustained and the programme of weight training on which he embarked in later life. Before the Master started having serious problems with his legs, he was initially quite sprightly, and enjoyed many diverse games with his disciples. I remember quite fondly Guru having us play tug-of-war, and he would often put one individual against another, or friends against friends. This also happened with country against country such as England against Germany or France, and Australia vs. New Zealand, or Canada vs. the United States.

How we laughed in those days! Sometimes enjoying the many, varied and excellent games played at the Aspiration-Ground. Some were imports from Guru's own native Bengal, while others were Western games, and the rest embellishments from him. Guru was extremely fond of laughter and of making his disciples laugh. For him, laughter had spiritual benefits, and it was one of the numerous tools or mediums that he used to make us happy. Sri Chinmoy had a series of performances called "Humour, My Only Saviour," and would often tell us many jokes. This he continued on vacations such as our annual Christmas Trip and other stop-overs to Sri Chinmoy Centres around the world. Below is a quote from Guru on humour:

"I am one of those who like humour. If you identify yourself with humour, you do not lose anything. It is like watching a child dancing in the playground, or playing in a garden; he is just jumping this side and that side. It is completely innocent." *Disciples Companion, Vol 2, P 10, (2006)*, Agni Press.

Humour was often used in his poems and aphorisms as well. He had a way of using words to teach us the inner life, which was extremely effective, imaginative, witty and fruitful. Here are two examples from a song and an aphorism:

"Disobedience, time is up!
Now you shut up!
Pack up!
And go away."

Disobedience Time is Up, (1994), Agni Press.

"Enthusiasm, enthusiasm, God's main food.
He begs me to eat, for my good."

– *Sri Chinmoy. Christmas Trip, December, 1999.* (Song)

Guru was also fond of saying "Bwa, Bwa," when he found something delightfully amusing, or more readily at the end of a special and excellent disciple performance, musical or otherwise. Of course disciples were all overjoyed to hear them, and for me in particular they were words which always thrilled my inner being. I believe that they were the Master's own words, but he generally used them – in my experience – when he was extremely pleased.

All my brief discussions with Sri Chinmoy were special and sacred. A quiet, contemplative man, he did not always speak or indulge in chat, preferring the approach of Questions and Answers to enlighten his many disciples. This was especially so in later years, when the disciple count grew and expanded all over the world. I remember speaking to Guru while in Scotland some years ago. He was talking on the phone via an international link-up with us, his students.

After thanking me for some aspect of the manifestation - the work that we do to serve the divinity within ourselves and others - I replied that I was striving to be a good instrument, to which He reassured me that I most certainly was. I immediately felt an inner thrill, delight and divine sense of pride. Such was the strength of his spiritual force. On another occasion he encouraged my return to my country, when I asked if it was fine to give classes on meditation there. Very soon afterwards, I visited Grenada and gave meditation classes in six different parishes.

Of course Sri Chinmoy, who played the role of a spiritual father, was also strict and sometimes exercised what he called his Justice or Justice-Light. Like any spiritual organisation, there are recommendations or 'rules' as we refer to them, which the Master sometimes used for helping

Me addressing an assembly at Starehe Boys School, Kenya, 2008. Sitting behind is Yohannes Tarekegn of Ethiopia, holding the Peace Torch. GregorKnauer is next to him. Both fellow Gurubhai's.

us to grow spiritually. This is something I knew of and which Sri Chinmoy had to do from time to time, for what I perceived to be spiritual reasons. Very occasionally disciples would be disciplined or get a scolding. This, in my case and others also, were welcome in so far as they often inspired us and helped us to grow more spiritually.

Others were less fortunate, but mostly we felt that Guru's Justice-Light was done out of Love and Compassion for us all, and was necessary and correct at the time. We knew that Guru did not compromise, that Obedience was necessary to maintain the beauty and fragrance of this extremely special Path. The following prose expresses this sentiment:

"If we follow the Will of our Inner Pilot, there is never any hesitation in our life. We must know that the moment an individual seeker obeys the Inner Pilot; a most beautiful rose comes into existence in the garden of God's Heart. This heart rose emanates a celestial fragrance that elevates the whole earth consciousness."

Talk given at Bristol University, England, July 16th, (1974). http://www. srichinmoy.org/resources/library/talks/inner_qualities/inner_obedience/ind   ex.html. Last visited 24th May, 2012.

How I loved listening to the Master! His voice, singing, presence, and all-knowing gaze gave me so much joy! He accepted me as I was with all my weaknesses, and gave me faith, strength, promise, hope and happiness. I could feel his blessings often, even when I was away from him and sometimes

as a consequence of my helplessness also. Indeed I feel fortunate as he has never really been far from me.

Sri Chinmoy's spiritual force was often manifested in the way he smiled. Guru had such sweetness in his many different shades of smiles, that numerous disciples commented upon them, and all felt helped in some way. For me they were smiles of joy, divine mischief, compassion, conveying Light or messages, suffering and Hope. As with his eyes, he could, and very often, did touch my Soul with one direct smile or look.

Sri Chinmoy, New York.

I also enjoyed the 'walk-by' or 'walk-past' meditations which he sometimes spontaneously did for the benefit of all. Here Sri Chinmoy would meditate while walking prayerfully and dynamically, sometimes at a moderate pace and also at a much faster pace. He would either go up and down the courtyard or circle the perimeter of the Aspiration-Ground. We, as disciples would simply sit and meditate.

The other way was when the Master would sit within or just outside the Aspiration- Ground Temple in a contemplative mood. Disciples would then walk by slowly and soulfully with folded hands, while going past the Master. This we did a few times, probably determined by the number of us and the logistics of accommodating so many in a small enclave. Our mode of walking was either in a circular fashion or in vertical rows as the occasion allowed, always walking past our Guru who continually gave us a loving gaze.

He could also be serious and would scold where necessary. This was my own individual and personal experience. With eyes that were usually half-open or closed, Guru had an indescribable physical presence, more so when he was in the deep contemplative state. Those affectionate and loving eyes seemed to have the capacity to pierce one's Soul and permeate the deepest part of being, all the way down to the physical body. He never seemed to miss a moment.

Sri Chinmoy sometimes scolded me, either personally, or through group talks given to all his students. I was always keen to hear his talks and to listen to his scolding's, for I learned much from them. Once in a while I would get messages sent to me in response to questions I asked, and they all inspired me immensely. Again, I found that even if I got the answer from someone else, his message was still infused with tremendous power, shifting obstacles from within.

Sri Chinmoy also blessed me quite a few times in a personal way, many of those blessings coming on my birthday. They also happened in a tangible way through flowers, gifts, my Soul's name, (Manatita), through food, and other ways. He even composed my name song, and sang it to me in my presence. My Soul's name's meaning as given by Sri Chinmoy is: - Beyond the mind – In

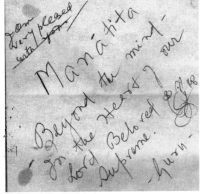

My Soul's name as given by Sri Chinmoy

the Heart of our Lord Beloved Supreme. A Soul's name represents the potentiality of the Soul, or if you like, the general direction that the soul wishes to take for its own inner experiences on the journey of life.

Every year we would visit Sri Chinmoy in New York, as April 13th, the day that he came to the West, and August 27th, his birthday, are very sacred to us. On some of our earlier visits, Sri Chinmoy's scoldings were more frequent. He also answered more questions on the spiritual life. Of course we learnt a lot from both, and took with us great inspiration upon returning to our individual countries.

The Master did not like unnecessary mixing of boys and girls[1], unless it was absolutely necessary, and for the manifestation of what Guru sometimes referred to as the 'Supreme'. (See Chapter 13). This was his preferred name for God, the Ultimate Reality; the Perennial Source from which all things come, live and have their Being. He was particularly careful with disciple 'dances' (bodily interpretations to music) during performances, and once said that he came from the 'No dancing school.' Nevertheless, as God is not bound by plans, He also is not bound by rules, and I have known Guru to allow dancing of a very refined, pure and devotional movement to invoke the blessings of Sri Krishna and other Masters who have passed on.

In an earthly way, Guru was an excellent, kind and noble Father. Yet again in a spiritual way, I always thought of him as the Universal Father. Someone who cared, not only for me, but was over-seeing the growth, and taking responsibility for the upliftment of all mankind. In that sense, I think of him as Love. "God is love" says St Paul in the Biblical scriptures, "and he that dwelleth in God dwelleth in Love." *The Bible, King James Version. 1 John 4: 16*

Again our Guru says that "He who loves never grows old. God is a shining example." *God's Hour, (1973), Agni Press.*

The Father cannot help but love the son, as the son is his own creation. Even so the universe is a creation of God, and God's Advocates cannot help but give their all for the glory of God in all. "If we can have love for the whole world1, we will have abiding peace." *CNN's Q &A with Riz Khan; May 21st, (1999).* Such Love as Sri Chinmoy gave; I can feel even on my darkest days!

I have written about Sri Chinmoy's Path in Chapter eleven, but I feel here that a glimpse into his ways would express his personality even more. Sri Chinmoy believed in speed. In any given moment we are living in the Eternal Now, and so speed was important to him. This was especially so for his disciples, as noted in one of his many admonitions:

"Why waste time, time is so precious while I am on Earth"

— *Sri Chinmoy.*

Guru was working day and night in many different fields of endeavour. For him, change of work is rest. He often said that in the spiritual life, there is no Saturday or Sunday. We should not take rest; for it is when we take rest that the forces of frustration and destruction find it easier to attack us. This the Master demonstrated every day of his life, and indeed I understand that he was holding functions and discourses even up to the last evening of his earthly sojourn.

In his so-called 'free' time, Guru was either painting or singing or talking to his disciples. At other times he would scribble on a notepad or draw another one of his millions of bird drawings. He was also fond of shopping and enjoyed bargaining as much as anyone else. He told us many tales about his shopping encounters, and wrote some short stories about them too.

Guru also did not lay emphasis on plans. "God is not bound by plans", he used to say. The Supreme can and does change His plan from time to time. I have experienced firsthand how some of our concerts and other meeting plans were changed by Sri Chinmoy and always for the better. He used to say that if you have flexible ideas, if you are adjustable to circumstances, then it is infinitely easier to manifest the Truth.

This gentle unassuming man was always positive. He saw the good of the world, its evolution and the part that we all have to play. To him we are not progressing from darkness to light, but from a lesser light to a greater Light. Seen in a more profound sense, ultimately, everything is one, and the word "Oneness" echoes over and over again in all of Sri Chinmoy's teachings.

I noticed his affection for, and ease with animals, and his childlike sweetness when singing for and playing with them. There were two dogs called Kanu and Chela of which he was extremely fond, and I once saw a video in which Guru behaved in a very tender and innocent way singing to, holding and hugging two dogs to the delight of his disciples.

Guruji had a burning intensity to serve others, and inspired this spirit of service in all his disciples. He has said that:

"To serve and never be tired is Love",
My Rose-Petals, Part 1, (1971), Agni Press.

That service was very often on a global scale. Nevertheless, I remember the little ways of service with Guru cooking for us and serving with his own hands. How sweet were the days at the Aspiration-Temple, where we sat down on the ground, waiting for Guru to serve us on banana leaves, and finally eating with our fingers, instead of knives and forks.

Sri Chinmoy instilled within us confidence, divine courage and the ability to believe in ourselves. For him impossibility is only in the mind. He often told us never to give up. Our only aim is progress, not victory or defeat:

"The determination in your heroic effort will permeate your mind and heart even after your success or failure is long forgotten." *Ten Thousand Flower-Flames, Part 98, (1983),* Agni Press.

This particular aphorism several disciples enjoyed printing on their T-shirts, and wearing at Marathons and other public events.

Failure occurs only when we give up, and Guru attempted to show us that message in his many failed attempts at trying to lift heavy weights. Here he faltered several times before succeeding. Of course he encouraged us in the Manifestation, (see Chapter eleven) and I would say that as a result of his inspiration, a lot of us have tried many times at achieving something great. Though we weathered many storms and failures before succeeding, we NEVER GAVE UP!

In the company of Guru, we enjoyed boat rides, train rides and pleasant walks. In his later years, when ailment prevented him from moving around as he wanted to, Sri Chinmoy would ride on specially designed buggy carts and three-wheelers or simply drive slowly around in his delightfully dainty and petite car. He appeared slower and moved with careful steps. At such times he would utilise the opportunity to do a walk- by meditation which, based on his highest experiences and inner depth, Guru would declare to be most effective.

It seemed to me, that whatever the Master did was designed for our own growth, since he himself had already achieved the Goal of life. This goal I will cover in the Chapter on *Love, Devotion And Surrender,* (Chapter eleven) but it is documented in Guruji's writings. I should point out, though, that Guruji did not speak so much of himself but of the Supreme, and only on rare occasions, identified himself with something Higher. So for example he would say: 'I am not this body, I am something else.' This last sentence is so aptly covered in the inspirational prose called *"Realise Me"*. This is available from Sri Chinmoy's disciples.

At intimate moments with Sri Chinmoy, he would tell us stories of his early years growing up in the Sri Aurobindo Ashram, and of his mischievous encounters with his family and friends. Sometimes Guru would carry on for a long time and afterwards apologise sweetly for keeping us so long. At other times He would pause and say 'Go and eat.' Of course few people moved as we suspected - nearly always correctly - that Sri Chinmoy would continue. What love the Master had for us! He would often tell us 'cock and bull' stories about India, the Ashram, his parents in heaven, and even his present encounters with the great Masters: Sri Ramakrishna, Lord Buddha, Lord Christ and others.

Guruji had a loving way of throwing Prasad – blessed food – at us, after or during a function, and would jokingly tease those who were not able to catch it. More often than not in those playful times and perhaps while rubbing his head, shaking his knees, or having his painful legs massaged, he would still tell us stories and jokes, teasing some 'favourite' disciples as well, and we would all bubble with happiness. He used to say that a certain favourite disciple of his had realised God and told funny stories about him. All present would then laugh out loud at the disciple's expense. Many a time boys and boys, or girls and girls would arm-wrestle or play marbles in innocent competition in Sri Chinmoy's presence.

So why was my Guru so revered and loved internationally? What made Kings and Presidents consult with Him? For what reason did Mohammed Ali, Jesse Owens, Leonard Bernstein and Pablo Casals treasure his presence and why did so many religious and spiritual leaders of different faiths feel honoured to be with him? Each question must be answered in a personal way. What I have observed is that many of these distinguished people felt totally at ease in his presence. They felt at ease because he treated them as true friends.

An inner virtue noticed by many was the Master's tremendous purity. The guests could feel it radiating from his eyes, face, smile, words and actions. Judging from their numerous comments, many felt that his life was not only extraordinary but exemplary. They saw how he reached out to them soulfully and sacredly without intentions or expectations, and they were enamoured by what they saw. Above all, they saw him as a servant of God. Even to this very day, they still visit us as guests and cannot stop telling us how much they loved Sri Chinmoy.

Dressed simply in one of his many beautifully coloured Dhotis (an Indian garment), Sri Chinmoy travelled around the world giving Peace Concerts, meeting many distinguished people. He wisely chose many different mediums, thus enabling him to reach humanity everywhere. This he did through weightlifting, sports and literature, music, humanitarian aid or the Sri Chinmoy Oneness-Home Peace Run/World Harmony Run, not forgetting his numerous paintings, art and drama through his accomplished plays.

Davao, Phillipines, 1993

Based on my own humble understanding of Sri Chinmoy's writings, it seemed to me that, seen from a spiritual perspective, cleverness was sometimes wisdom. It was necessary to bring to the fore not only our own good qualities, but the good qualities of others.

"Wisdom-light is absolutely necessary in the spiritual life so that you can avoid misunderstandings and unhappiness" *Sri Chinmoy Answers, Part 18, (1999),* Agni Press.

This wisdom-cleverness-light my Master was to continue to utilise to the fullest in dealing with others, until his Mahasamadhi – a God-man's conscious exit from this world - on October 11th, 2007.

- Manatita, December, 2007.

CHAPTER SIX

The Human Psyche

"Your soul has a special mission. Your soul is supremely conscious of it. *Maya*, illusion or forgetfulness, makes you feel that you are finite, weak and helpless. This is not true. You are not the body. You are not the senses. You are not the mind. These are all limited. You are the soul, which is unlimited. Your soul is infinitely powerful. Your soul defies all time and space …

Your special mission - which is the fulfilment of your divinity - is not outside you, but within you. Search within. Meditate within. You will discover your mission." *Yoga And The Spiritual Life. The Journey of India's Soul, Section 1, (1971),* Agni Press.

Before we go deeper into Sri Chinmoy's teachings, it is perhaps necessary to understand the *Human Psyche, the* progressive stages of consciousness that make up the human personality and beyond.

Soulful homage to Kamakura Buddha, 1992

Sri Chinmoy speaks of the Body, Vital, Mind, Heart and finally the Soul. This in no way takes away from the western concept of Body and Soul, but indeed enhances it as Sri Chinmoy elucidates his teachings. As these words will be re-visited again, let us look at them one by one:

The **Body**, according to Sri Chinmoy, has inexhaustible potential, as it's a gift of God, the Supreme. The body houses the Soul and indeed, before realisation, the body helps the Soul. After realisation, the body serves the Soul in order to manifest the divine. The Soul needs the body to have a place to live; to manifest its qualities here on earth. According to Sri Chinmoy, the body offers its capacity in service; the Soul offers its capacity in meditation. In this way, they both go together perfectly. The following prose clarifies this quite well:
"For the realisation of the highest and deepest Truth, the body needs the soul; for the manifestation of the highest and deepest Truth, the soul needs the body" *Beyond Within, P. 19, (1985),* Agni Press.

"We may call the body a temple. Inside the temple is the shrine, the heart. Within the shrine is the deity, the Soul. Now let us speak only of the soul and the body, since that is your question. Body and soul are like a house and its owner. The soul is the owner and the body is the house. The soul and the body are complimentary. Without the soul, without the owner, the house is useless. The soul works inside the body, as well as with the body, through the body and for the body consciousness. Again, without the body, the soul will have no place to live. It will not be able to manifest its qualities on earth. When the owner is there and the body is in perfect condition, then the message of the soul can be revealed and manifested." *(ibid. p. 20).*

The **Vital** is the second member of this psyche. According to Sri Chinmoy, it has a dynamic and stupendous inner urge, without which nothing can be embodied or revealed here on earth. I tend to associate it with a positive inner drive that enables me to accomplish great things in life.

"Yours is the indomitable courage that springs from the fountain of boundless emotion", says Sri Chinmoy. "With the infinite Blessings of the Supreme, on you march across the path of Infinity's bloom, Eternity's glow and Immortality's lustre. Your life is green, the ever-aspiring and ever-growing green. Your breath is blue, the ever-encompassing and ever-transforming blue. O vital of mine, in you is humanity's glowing hope. With you is Divinity's reverberating clarion." *(Ibid. p. 29).*

Unfortunately, as well as divine dynamism, the Vital also embodies hostile aggression. It is the soul's light coming to the fore that changes the hostile aggression into divine dynamism.

In Sri Chinmoy's teachings, there is a lower aspect of our Vital which he calls 'the lower vital.' It is the seat of conscious and unconscious demands and expectations. These forces come from a very low plane of consciousness, and are often identified with human love where there are fears, insecurities, lusts, doubts and many more. The lower vital is the part of us that has not yet been touched by the divine light; not yet illumined. It is the animal side of our nature. Here one's love is impure and one wrestles with gigantic forces of ignorance. Speaking of the lower vital plane, Sri Chinmoy says that it is:

"Unlit, impure, frightening and threatening. It tempts us to lead a very undivine and corrupted life ... A vital demand is always destructive. It does not embody any light, and at the same time it does not care for light" *(ibid. p. 39)*

It is the heart's purifying and transforming love, entering into the lower vital, which will allow it to become a most significant instrument of the Supreme.

The Mind is seen both from the physical and spiritual standpoint. The physical mind is caught up in the gross physical consciousness. The spiritual mind, the illumined mind, because of its capacity to stay in the aspiring heart, is able to see and grow into the higher truth. One understands from Sri Chinmoy's Yoga, that the ordinary mind is not only afraid of vastness, but doubts its very existence. When the mind is attacked by jealousy, fear and doubt, these forces make it feel useless; then ego enters and feeds the mind.

"The human mind cares for aesthetic beauty, for poise and balance," says Sri Chinmoy. "The human mind is searching for Truth, for Light, for Reality. But unfortunately, it wants to see the highest Truth in its own limited way. It does not want to transcend itself to reach the ultimate Truth. Furthermore, the physical mind wants to examine the highest Truth, which is absurd." *(Ibid. p. 44)*.

Sri Chinmoy recognises the paramount importance of the human mind in separating us from the animal kingdom through the process of cosmic evolution, something necessary for the blossoming of the human life. However, with the help of the soul, it is the spiritual mind that wants to go "far, far beyond the domain of reason, in order to see, feel and grow into the ultimate, transcendental Truth." *(Ibid)*.

In Sri Chinmoy's Yoga, the ordinary mind is restless and limited. Its very nature is to analyse, to chop things up, and to separate. The Master tells us that it is 'forever on the move.' The mind is involved with thinking and thinking, with confusion, doubts and endless questions. However, when it is illumined through the light of meditation, by spiritual practices, as facilitated by the soul's inner will, then that inner glow will permeate our outer actions. Sri Chinmoy says it best:

> "When we enter into the totally dark, unlit obscure room of action with our mental plan, it is like carrying a candle. But when we enter into the room with our soul's light, the room is flooded with illumination." (*Ibid. p. 47*).

We see here also that the mind is full of promise, as Sri Chinmoy calls upon it to:

"Don the golden robes of simplicity, sincerity and purity. Permit not the gales of disbelief to extinguish your inner mounting flame. Yours is the arrow of concentration. Yours is the soil of lightning intuition. Yours is the unhorizoned peace." *(Ibid. p. 45)*.

The Heart follows an upward progression, just as the previous members do. It is sometimes associated with mundane emotions, but the Master's writings speak of it as being free from worry and doubt. It is also full of selfless love, and has a pure longing which gives it immediate access to the Supreme. It is the nature of the heart to identify itself with the Highest, with the farthest, with the inmost. It thinks in terms of expansion: 'we' and 'ours' and not 'me' and 'mine.

The Master speaks of the heart as being faster, safer and surer than any other road. The heart's qualities are like those of a child: innocence, purity, love, simplicity, spontaneity and oneness. "Oneness with Light, oneness with Truth and oneness with inner beauty." Says Sri Chinmoy. *(Ibid. p. 69)*.

In one of his many lofty and poetic utterances on the heart, Sri Chinmoy says:

> "Yours is the unfaltering will and unfailing faith in the Supreme. Each petal of the radiant lotus deep within you is perpetually bathed in nectar-rays of the Transcendental Delight. O sweet, sweeter, sweetest heart of mine, you are not only God's. God also is yours." *(ibid. p. 64)*

The heart is full of sympathy and concern, and it is all harmony. The heart expands, and it is inside the heart that the soul abides. Sri Chinmoy feels that it is only by meditating on the heart that one can contact the soul. In the

Master's teaching, this spiritual heart – not physical – is located in the centre of the chest, in the centre of our existence.

"The Soul is the final member of the human psyche. It comes into birth for experience, and its experience will be complete when it brings down all the perfection of the Divine into matter. Each soul needs involution and evolution. When the soul descends, it is the soul's involution. When the soul ascends, it is the soul's evolution. The soul enters into the lowest abyss of inconscience. The soul evolves again into Satchidananda. Existence-Consciousness-Bliss. The triple consciousness." *(ibid. p. 81).*

I have already mentioned the soul in conjunction with the Body and the Heart. The soul is the highest member of the human psyche. Sri Chinmoy describes it as the 'King' and the heart as the 'Commander-in-chief.' The call of self-enquiry itself: "Who am I? "Where have I come from?" "For whom am I here on earth?" comes from the Soul. The Soul needs to achieve absolute fulfilment here on earth, precisely because it is the self-effulgent messenger of God within. It is eternal and immortal. It migrates from body to body, in the process of re-incarnation. It knows no birth, no decay and no death: The soul is part and parcel of God Itself:

> "It is absolutely correct that the soul has neither beginning nor end. It is constantly progressing and moving towards its Goal. It has infinite potentialities because it is part of the Self. In our *Gita*, we have the most sublime description of the soul: "The soul is ancient, permanent, eternal, immutable and all-pervading. Weapons cannot cleave it. Fire cannot burn it. Water cannot drench it. The wind cannot dry it." This is the description of the soul given by the Lord, Sri Krishna" *Earth's Cry Meets Heaven's smile, Part 2, Section 1, (1974),* Agni Press.

The soul utilises the body to manifest and fulfil God in an unprecedented way. It wants to reveal and manifest its divinity – Light, Peace, Bliss and Power – here on earth. Each soul is unique, according to Sri Chinmoy, and has its particular divine mission to fulfil only through that particular soul. We have to welcome our soul and unite ourselves with it, for it is only by so doing, that fear, ignorance and death, will finally leave us, and Eternity, Infinity and Immortality will welcome us here on Earth and there in Heaven.

- Manatita 14th May, 2012

CHAPTER SEVEN

A Glimpse Into The Self-Transcendence of Sri Chinmoy

"We use the term 'transcendental Consciousness'; again, we speak of the ever-transcending transcendental Consciousness. The transcendental Consciousness, *Turiya*, is the highest, but this transcendental Consciousness is not static. It is also constantly transcending itself. God is infinite, eternal and immortal; but all spiritual Masters know that God is also ever-progressing. God Himself is in the process of evolution. He is making progress, constant progress, in and through everyone in order to establish perfect Perfection on earth."- Sri Chinmoy. *Transformation-Night, Immortality-Dawn, (1975), Agni Press*

Meditation in Rhode Island, 1984. By Niriha.

The above quote expresses beautifully, Sri Chinmoy's inner realisation on Self- transcendence. One's life has no end; one's life-march knows no halt. Life is an eternal journey, and so the real in one goes one step ahead. There is no final destination as such, for one's destination becomes 'the starting point for the next day's journey.' Consider this vivid description below:

"Today we are at the starting point. Tomorrow we reach our destination. The day after tomorrow, that destination becomes the starting point for a higher goal, a more fulfilling goal. There is no absolute goal; the goal is always transcending its own supernal heights" *The Oneness of the Eastern Heart and the Western Mind, Pt. 2, P 464. (2004).* Agni Press.

Sri Chinmoy says that when we look at God the Dream from various angles, we call them realities, but actually, it is a dream which is in the process of blossoming into reality. What we think of as reality does not exist in the inner world. There is only Dream. This he expresses most powerfully in the following imagery:

".... It is like a tree that produces countless leaves, flowers and fruits. The Tree, which is God, embodies the universal Dream and also the individual  Dreams. So God Himself is the Dream that is blossoming at every moment, the Dream that embodies Eternity's Vision, Infinity's Heart and Immortality's Life. This dream has its will-power, eagerness, vision, creation, manifestation... everything." *Disciple's Companion, Vol 6 P. 107, (2004)*. Agni Press.

To manifest that dream, the Master feels that what is necessary from the seeker, is constant inner hunger, the recognition of the supreme truth that at every moment, he is transcending his own highest height by "virtue of his self-giving to the ever- transcending Reality and Divinity." *Oneness of The Eastern Heart And The Western Mind, Vol 3, P. 107, (2004)*. Agni Press.

A Contemplative-looking Sri Chinmoy

This inner hunger Sri Chinmoy calls Aspiration. Once one transcends the life of conscious impurity and obscurity, the life of desire, he is living the life of Aspiration. It is this aspiration, according to the Master, that takes the seeker high, higher, highest, on the strength of his inner mounting cry: (see Chapter eleven)

"Each time our aspiration, our mounting cry, touches the highest pinnacle, it is fired again. The goal that it touches, need not, and cannot be the ultimate goal, for today's goal is tomorrow's starting point. Again, tomorrow's goal will be the starting point for the day after tomorrow. There is no end to our realisation. There is no end to our self-transcendence. Our aspiration ascends, our realisation transcends. Our satisfaction dawns and finally, our

God smiles. With our inner cry, we ascend to God's descending smile. When we feed our inner cry and when we become our inner cry, at that time our song of realisation and transcendence begins." *(Ibid, pt 2, p. 355).*

In pursuing the spirit of self-transcendence, lies the message of happiness and great joy in boundless measure. This one can utilise, even in the spirit of competition:

"When we transcend ourselves, we do not compete with others. We do not compete with the rest of the world, but at every moment, we compete only with ourselves, with our previous achievements. And each time we surpass our previous achievements, we get joy." *(Ibid, Vol. 3, p. 119).*

One sees this spirit of Self-Transcendence manifested in Sri Chinmoy's own life. This was demonstrated most significantly in his sporting accomplishments, whether it was playing tennis, even in his seventies, lifting unprecedented weights, or in his art, literature, music and many other fields of endeavour.

So why did he pursue such goals? Sri Chinmoy saw himself as an eternal seeker. But perhaps more significantly, he demonstrated those great Truths in his life to inspire his disciples and to serve humanity. He saw that having a fixed goal meant that there is a finishing point, whereas one's true goal is always to make continuous progress. Being satisfied with success is rather like putting an end to the journey. He wanted us to "maintain a conscious feeling for the Supreme... because you are marching toward an eternal goal." *Sri Chinmoy Speaks, Part 7, P. 22-25, (1976),* Agni Press.

"Every day you have to feel that you have a higher goal. Do not think that yesterday's is the final goal in your life. When you have a fixed goal and you reach it, this is your success. Then you are finished; after that you are not doing anything. But if you do not have a fixed goal, you are going on constantly. Then you are making progress and in continuing progress, your goal is constantly going beyond, beyond, beyond. At that time you get the greatest satisfaction." *(Ibid).*

All life flows, like a river. Perfection is part of the process. It is not, and cannot be a finished product, as stated by Sri Chinmoy. It cannot be an ultimate height that defies transcendence. Rather it "is something that constantly transcends its own reality, its own height, and its own goal. Perfection is like a river that flows constantly to the ever-expanding, ever-transcending sea. It is not like a stagnant pool or lake; it is a dynamic river that flows towards the ever-transcending beyond." *The Oneness of The Eastern Heart And The Western Mind, Vol 3, p.17, (2004).* Agni Press.

In the divine scheme of things, there are no fixed goals. This is a message that is repeated time and time again in all aspects of the Master's work. Perfection is not a set standard, but a continuous progress:

"Perfection is the seeker's divinely surrendered self-expansion in God's illumining satisfaction and fulfilling manifestation. Perfection is self-transcendence. It is the art of piloting Eternity's Boat in Infinity's Sea towards Immortality's Shore. Perfection is self-giving. Perfection is the flower which grows into a God-nourishing fruit" *(Ibid. p. 29).*

"Realisation is something that constantly transcends itself. It is the pathfinder of a higher and deeper goal." says Sri Chinmoy. There is no end to our realisation:

"God is eternal. Our Journey is eternal, and the road that we are marching on is also eternal. We are eternal divine soldiers marching towards the beyond that is constantly transcending its own boundary." *(Ibid. Pt. 2, p.112).*

Expressed as only Sri Chinmoy can do, is the triune of realisation, revelation and manifestation. Here he indicates that none are finished products:

"Inside realisation is the ever-mounting inner cry, the ever-transcending expansion of consciousness, and the conscious expansion of the limited self into the divine self. Similarly, inside revelation is the constant inner urge to reveal Eternity's Goal. And inside manifestation is realisation and revelation; so in manifestation, there is also the same process. It is an endless process of the universal self-transcendence." *(Ibid. Pt. 1, p.8, (2003).* He continues:

"Manifestation is preparatory to perfection, and perfection is the song of eternal transcendence... Perfection is constantly in the process of transcending its own height." (Ibid. p. 100).

So one sees here that realisation is the pathfinder to a higher and deeper Goal; that God is eternal. Our journey is eternal, and the road that one is marching on is also eternal. All are divine soldiers marching towards the beyond that is constantly transcending its own boundary." *Ibid. Pt 2, p.112, (2004).*

Sri Chinmoy's philosophy has been applied in a very dynamic way by his sporting students. Some have climbed mountains. A feat that many of them had not dared to do before meeting Sri Chinmoy, and grasping the beauty of his philosophy. Others have run across the desert, taken part in ultra-marathons and one has swum the English Channel a staggering ten times! Sri Chinmoy's philosophy can be applied to every home and in all fields of endeavour.

"You can always do more," he says. "Today's goal is only the starting point for tomorrow's new dawn. At every moment we are transcending our previous achievements ... our goal should be our own progress, and progress itself is the most illumining experience." *The Outer Running and the Inner Running, p.17, (1984).* Agni Press.

Sri Chinmoy, who left this world 76 years young in 2007, was a most perfect example of his teachings. Originally a sprinter, this athletic Guru began making his transition to longer races in 1978. He ran his first marathon nine months later, and within two years, had completed 9 marathons, two ultra-marathons, plus a dozen or so other events. He was then 48 yrs. old. Back in his native India, between the ages of twelve to thirty-two, Sri Chinmoy was the decathlon champion for 2 years in the spiritual community in which he lived. He was also the area's fastest runner, winning the 100 metre dash for a remarkable seventeen times!

Sri Chinmoy's vision is that we all have unlimited potential. Nothing is impossible if we can go beyond the barriers created by our own mind. To bring our capacities to the fore, we need faith, discipline and the determination never, never to give up! Life is not made for failure but for progress. No matter how many times we try and fail, we should never give up! Eventually, nature itself will surrender to our determination.

The Master taught that sports bring dynamism and power into the body and that physical fitness is of great importance in one's life. A body in good condition enables all life's activities to be done well. Consequently, daily physical exercise, seen from his standpoint, is very important, in order to perform life's duties well. If one is strong, healthy and dynamic, if one is physically fit, one can keep ailments and uninvited guests from entering one's being. *(Ibid. p.143). (1998).*

This synthesis of outer fitness, accompanied by inner fitness through meditation, is present throughout the teachings and activities of this sport philosopher and champion athlete. In the act of competing, he says, we strive only to surpass our previous standard. The other athlete is necessary, but only to bring out the best in us. Success and failure are simply experiences that come to one along the way. One can go beyond them. This indomitable urge to transcend is expressed thus:

> "The determination in your heroic effort will permeate your hearts and minds even after your success or failure, is long forgotten." *Seventy-Seven Thousand Service-Trees, Part 13, (1999),* Agni Press.

And on competition:

> "We compete not for the sake of defeating others, but in order to bring forward our own capacity. Our best capacity comes forward, only when there are other people around us. They inspire us to bring forward our utmost capacity, and we inspire them to bring forward theirs. That is why we have competitive sports. The seeker-athlete never tries to compete with others, but only tries to transcend his capacity." *The Outer Running and the Inner Running, P141, (1984).* Agni Press.

Self-transcendence, for Sri Chinmoy, indicates a natural evolutionary drive that is part of the Earth itself. All levels of the earth creation, he teaches, are striving consciously or unconsciously to improve. When this striving is conscious through meditation, progress is made more quickly. Physical fitness is the quickest and simplest means to bring the qualities of endurance into an individual consciousness, and as such is heavily emphasised.

Sri Chinmoy excelled in many sports, including soccer, volleyball, table-tennis and tennis, an event he played well into his sixties. He also applied the same vigour to weightlifting. Sri Chinmoy majored in numerous works of art, paintings, music, poetry and writings. He wrote nearly 1600 books, painted nearly 200,000 works of art, and composed over 20,000 devotional songs. He gave over 750 concerts, playing on nearly 100 instruments varying from flutes, harmonium, and piano, to Indian sitar and esraj.

Today, the Sri Chinmoy Marathon Team are at work in over 200 centres, in over 60 countries throughout the world, providing the public with over 500 races a year. The team's longest race is an elite invitational 3100 mile race in New York. They are also famous for their Self-transcendence races, (previously called *Runners are Smilers*), held mostly on a one mile loop throughout many countries around the world. Acting on the inspiration from Sri Chinmoy, the team tries to bring forward the inner capacities of the runner such as cheerfulness; courage, endurance, and the determination to transcend his/her own capacities.

Playing the esraj. Peace Concert, 1990. Sri Lanka.

Sri Chinmoy applied that same sporting philosophy towards the Olympics. For the athlete, it represents a great opportunity and possibility to transcend his own capacities, to inspire humanity to achieve, and to raise its standard:

> "A true gain and a true achievement for the whole world, for increasing the capacity and standard of the world. The athlete's goal should be his own continuous progress, if he can continuously transcend his own achievements; he is bound to achieve satisfaction" *(Ibid. pp. 155-156).*

This Chapter concludes with two inspirational sayings from Sri Chinmoy:

> "Determination can change your mind.
> Determination can change your heart.
> Determination can change your life all together."

-Sri Chinmoy.

"Every day, when morning dawns, we should feel that we have something new to accomplish. We are running, and every day we are advancing. If we are aspiring, we are always in the process of running. When we start our journey in the morning, we should feel that today is the continuation of yesterday's journey; we should not take it as a totally new beginning. And tomorrow we should feel that we have travelled still another mile." *(Ibid. p. 19).*

-Manatita, 2010

CHAPTER EIGHT

A Glimpse Into Sri Chinmoy's Vision of America

"O green-blue Sacred Fire, O Sun Freedom-Light,

O Heaven's gold Delight,

America, O my child of speed,

My Supreme Promise-Seed." –Sri Chinmoy.

The Sacred Fire, Act 2, Scene 4, (1975), Agni Press

In this chapter, I will attempt to share with you, my reader, the vision of America as seen through the eyes of Sri Chinmoy. In doing so, however, it is necessary that I discuss four essential truths, which he felt contributed greatly to the development of America:

1. The Founding Fathers, poets, patriotic heroes and seers, were paramount to the true worth, sacrifice, lofty ideals and self-giving of America. They also contributed to the progressive spirit, speed and advancement of their country. Sri Chinmoy's supreme utterance below serves to remind us of this:

    "The Supreme had a special vision for the soul of America, and He revealed it first through the Founding Fathers." *I Need My Country: Beauty's Soul, Section 1, (1975),* Agni Press.

2. To have an understanding of America from Sri Chinmoy's standpoint, it is important to recognise that it has a Soul. The Soul is the divine spark that creates its reality and embodies its vision for the future. Sri Chinmoy teaches us that:

    "Every Nation has its soul. The Soul of a nation consists of its aspirations, aptitudes and capacities placed at the service of the Supreme" He continues: "Judging by her history, America holds the brightest promise of placing at the service of the Divine, her aspirations, aptitudes and capacities, as she has often, in times of need, placed them at the service of humanity" *I Love my Country: Purity's Body, Section1, (1975),* Agni Press.

Sri Chinmoy's natural clarity of the Soul and its beauty is expressed below:

"The soul of America, like a child, is growing, glowing, developing, illumining and fulfilling. It is a soul that is most progressive and most striking" *The Bicentennial Flames at the United Nations,* Section 1, (1976), Agni Press.

3.   *The Sacred Fire,* from which some of my thoughts have come, was written in 1975. Nevertheless, Sri Chinmoy saw his vision of America, long before touching down on its soil on April 13th, 1964. Indeed, it was for this reason that he came. He felt that India's vision and America's vision ran parallel, and while both countries were sometimes at odds with one another, they "basically love each other, for each have the self-same goal: A peaceful life." *The Sacred Fire, Act V1, Scene1, P52, (1975), reprinted 1998, Madal Bal.*

Sending of a peace dove, Ellis Island

4.   There was a profound relationship between England and America, which to an extent, assisted with the shape and growth of the two countries. In *The Sacred Fire,* Sri Chinmoy writes lovingly of England as the Mother and America as the daughter. The Mother is of 'exquisite beauty', and the daughter has 'indomitable strength.' Indeed the Soul of America manifested mostly through power. As the Soul of America matured, it felt the need to take care of itself. In Sri Chinmoy's eloquent and poetic way, he describes America's striving for self-advancement thus:

"...There is a beauty in the rising sun and there is a beauty in the setting sun, equally charming, illumining and fulfilling. You (England) have so far enjoyed the beauty of the rising sun, but from now on, you will have to enjoy the beauty of the setting sun. And you, my brave America, before long you shall start enjoying the beauty of the rising sun .... the sun that illumines, the sun that liberates, the sun that immortalises the soul and the body of aspiring humanity ....." (*Ibid. Act 1, Scene 2, p.14*).

Both countries eventually came to be happy with and in each other, sharing many heartfelt qualities together, including England's nobility, and America's self-giving heart. Before returning to the Founding Fathers, I would like to sum up with one soul-stirring quote on America by Sri Chinmoy:

"O Dignity-Majesty-Divinity-reality-flooded Soul of American Liberty! These are the good, better, best qualities of the real America, the America which is to raise the consciousness of the world, and why I came here. This is the America I envisioned in India. "Beautiful" – the real Beauty of the Absolute Supreme, universal Beauty of the Supreme, America the country embodies.

America is the land of hope, the land of promise. There will be countless Americans who will be able to bask in the sunshine of America's divine reality. America means not only the West but the entire globe" On America. Courtesy of *http://us.srichinmoycentre.org* (Last visited 5th April, 2010.)

In Sri Chinmoy's writings, the self-giving of the Founding Fathers was for something higher and deeper. In the deepest recesses of their hearts, they wanted to manifest a higher truth, to show that liberty was not only for them, but for the use of the entire world. According to Sri Chinmoy, Light always has to be embodied by great individuals. It was Thomas Jefferson's vision and of all those who surrounded him – Washington, Adams, Franklyn, Paine, Munro and others.

There was also another wave of patriotism when Abraham Lincoln came. Patriots, in Sri Chinmoy's vision, are "those who have helped their country and elevated its consciousness so that the reality of their country has widened." He continues:

"The American patriots of the past felt that life and patriotism were inseparable. They felt that patriotism was the manifestation of life's freedom, that it was the only way to love one's country. And they did not expect anything from the country. They only wanted to give what they had and what they were" *I Need my Country: Beauty's Soul, Section 1, (1975),* Agni Press.

According to Sri Chnmoy, the Soul of America came forward to offer its light and delight to those brave souls, to inject the feeling of patriotism into those few selected children of America. By so doing, they were able to become true and humble instruments of God, pleasing God according to their capacity, understanding and their inner and outer awakening.

Thomas Jefferson and his Declaration of Independence, was one such vision. Sri Chinmoy writes that he was a 'good man. A God-messenger, a Vision-son of God.' He had 'clarity, luminosity and vastness', and in his case, 'mind, body, vital, heart, everything went together.' 'God gave him capacities in many walks of life and he used them well.' *I Love my Country: Purity's Body, Section1, (1975),* Agni Press.

Because it is so significant, I enclose below Sri Chinmoy's lofty utterance on the Declaration of Independence.

"The American Declaration of Independence had the pioneer vision of faith, dignity and humanity's basic needs: equal rights, justice and freedom. Clarity, luminosity and vastness, these the Declaration of Independence embodies. It is not a mere declaration. It is something infinitely more. It is the freedom-cry of humanity's aspiration-day from the frustration-night of ignorance" *The Bicentennial Flames at The United nations, (1976),* Agni Press.

Sri Chinmoy saw George Washington as 'the Father of the American Nation. He was the son of peace and the brother of self-giving.' He had the indomitable spirit of a General and the peerless wisdom of a President. He was also 'the first and last President to be everybody's choice.' Sri Chinmoy continues that his 'high character and majestic will, powerfully blend with courage and capacity.' *The Sacred Fire, Act 2, Scene 2, (1975),* Agni Press.

There were many other seers and patriots. Sri Chinmoy mentions Ralph Waldo Emerson's indomitable will and utter self-reliance, and described him as a 'prophet of Universal Faith, a seer visualising the future in the living present. 'Very few souls as Emerson have come into the world; he had light in abundant measure.' Whitman was 'the vision of the oneness of everything and in everything.' While Emerson was 'soft, sweet and luminous', Whitman 'dynamically fronted the Reality which is manifesting to an ever-increasing extent.' They were both, 'Fellow-pilgrims on their way to the Home of God, the culmination of today's world, they march in stupendous glory.' *Philosopher-Thinkers: The Power-Towers of the Mind and Poet-Seers: The Fragrance-Hours of the Heart in the West,* (1998), Agni Press.

Of course one would not speak of all these noble and God-given attributes without seeing how they have shaped America and its people. It has given her strength, vastness, a progressive spirit, courage, supernal beauty and matchless pomp. It has also given her an unimaginable speed for progress. 'Speed', that one quality that Sri Chinmoy loved so much:

"Always long for speed
If not the slow death of stagnation
Will capture you."

Seventy-Seven Thousand Service-Trees, Pt. 6, Poem 5754, Agni Press, (1998)

"Do not waste time Tomorrow never comes!" *Poem 49,299.*
"Each moment is precious
Extremely precious
Far beyond our imagination"
Poem 49,222.

To continue about America's great: Abraham Lincoln championed the equality of every man's birth right, and faith in God's justice. His Gettysburg address was incomparable:

"He had the gift to dream of union,
The courage and capacity to fight,
The confidence to win,
The patience that knew no flagging."

America in Her Depts. (1973), Agni Press.

John F. Kennedy was 'the Universal Heart':

"Prince of high idealism, Freedom incarnate,
Helper of humanity."

Kennedy: The Universal Heart, (1973), Agni Press.

He was eloquent in his Inaugural Address, "that soul-stirring address that is as deep as the Atlantic in its outlook; ideals as high as the Himalayas and resolutions as powerful as atomic power." *(Ibid).*

"President Kennedy is, as it were, the lineal descendant of the American nation's traditional leadership. As George Washington was the father of The United States, as Abraham Lincoln was its saviour, as Franklyn D Roosevelt was the Voice of America, even so is John F Kennedy the Noble Defender of World freedom and World Peace." *(Ibid)*.

Of course there were others and Sri Chinmoy said that there will be others whose inner experiences have awakened and will be awakening America, illumining and adding to America's consciousness. Sri Chinmoy has utilised his poetry, songs, aphorisms, prose and even America's symbols to honour such individuals and America itself. John Adams, that 'truth-fighter with a volcano-will', John Quincy Adams, whose 'heart cries to elevate the weak, to help the needy', Benjamin Franklin, 'the oldest and the wisest of all', all contributed to America's present consciousness. *The Sacred Fire, Act 4, Scene 3, (1975)*, Agni Press.

There were also Nathan Hale, 'Earth's colossal sacrifice and Heaven's hallowed satisfaction', Emily Dickinson who, with her 'heart's inner music, blessed America's children with glowing simplicity, purity and luminosity. She also gave to the American consciousness, a new dimension; a new type of soul-search –soft, delicate and lucid.' And Woodrow Wilson's sacrifice and contribution to the League of Nations, has added to the glories of America's hero-warriors that make her proud. *(Ibid)*.

Finally, it is worth mentioning that Sri Chinmoy showed a deep appreciation for the American Flag as embodying 'divine power, divine purity, divine vastness and spirituality' and as for the Motto: 'In God We Trust', he spoke of it as a Motto of the highest order. On America's sacred Liberty Torch, here is a most powerful aphorism:

> "Birthless are the flames of the Liberty Torch,
> Deathless is the light of the Liberty Torch.
> The Liberty Torch is a human aspiration,
> A divine realisation and supreme perfection"
> *The Liberty Torch, (1976)*, Agni Press.

"America is a young nation. It does not want to walk; it wants to run as fast as possible in order to breast the tape first. I appreciate America for its dynamism. If you are dynamic, you run towards your goal. If you do not know where the goal is, then you may run from this side to that side. But it is better than to remain static. Americans are running" *The Outer Running and the Inner Running, P160, (1984)* Agni Press.

The above prose, written in the early eighties, indicates that Sri Chinmoy saw America as a young nation. However, with all its powerful and unprecedented changes in recent times, one wonders as to how this ever-progressive teacher, would see America in the world of today. America means speed, he said. Speed to run the fastest. It is a dynamic country running towards its goal. *(Ibid)*.

Sri Chinmoy spoke of the beauty and inner urge of America many times from the seventies and all the way into the 21st Century. He compared it to representing the ideals of King Janaka – a wise King and seeker after knowledge - Prince Siddhartha – a loving prince about 2,500yrs ago, who later became the Buddha - and Emperor Asoka – a great Indian Emperor of the Maurya Dynasty in ancient times - he is said to have ruled for 63 years.

America utilised her vast wealth for the restoration of Europe, in her service of impoverished India, and in many other countries, large and small, it made her, 'in the modern context, stand forth uniquely as the most fit for the ideals of Janaka, Siddhartha and Asoka.' *Eternity's Breath, P105, (1972)*, Agni Press.

In Sri Chinmoy's view, America's munificence, her ever-progressive mind and the dynamism of her spirit, have been an asset to the whole international community.

Sri Chinmoy saw the process - the ever-evolving consciousness of America - moving rapidly forwards. It makes mistakes, but like the elephant which bounces against a wall, it picks itself up and continues to move. This spirit of Americans running is depicted below:

"They may not be sure of the goal, but they are constantly on the move. They go to one side and run into a wall and get hurt. Then they go to another side and the goal is not there, so they get another blow. But at least they go." *The Outer Running and the Inner Running, P160-161, (1984)*. Agni Press.

Speaking of the bicentennial presentation of "America the beautiful", Sri Chinmoy said that it gave him abundant joy, 'because there the soul and the spirit of America are embodied and represented in a most striking manner' *Aum Magazine, Vol 4, No 1, P16, (1977)*.

Here is a most appropriate poem expressing America's beauty:

O Beautiful America

"O Beautiful America of the Lord Supreme
You are the pride divine of our soul. The boundless glory of your giant arms And
the nectar-flood of your loving heart
Are but a collection of delight-flowers in the blue-vast sky."

Songs dedicated to America. Courtesy of *(http://us.srichinmoycentre.org)*. Last
visited 3rd July, 2010.

As previously mentioned, every nation has a soul. This is reflected in its aspirations, aptitudes and capacities placed at the service of the Supreme. Now that there is a spiritual awakening in the world, Sri Chinmoy felt that it was only a question of years before its golden glint falls on the face of every nation. When that happens, its hidden divinity will shine forth to a greater or lesser degree on everyone.

Judging from her history, towards that end, "America holds out the brightest promise of placing, at the service of the Divine, her aspirations, aptitudes and capacities, as she has often, in times of need, placed them at the service of humanity" *Eternity's Breath, (1972), P107,* Agni Press.

We see this futuristic vision and spiritual assertiveness of Sri Chinmoy expressed in three of his most striking utterances On America:

"The next two hundred years will see the manifestation of the soul's qualities of America. This manifestation will take place in America's conscious and unconditional leadership of humanity and America's constant and self-giving friendship with humanity"

"Undoubtedly the spiritual forces will be able to manifest in the next two hundred years much more than they did in the past two hundred years, for not only America's but also humanity's aspiration is continuously proceeding forward, upward and inward." *The Bicentennial Flames At The United Nations, (1976),* Agni Press.

"America will offer her unprecedented capacity
For the community of nations
And make all nations feel that
Her height and depth and speed and power
Are for them to claim as their very own,
And thus create a satisfying and satisfied world-family." *(Ibid).*

Sri Chinmoy was conscious that America had taken a major part in the economic rehabilitation of India. Interestingly enough, this helps Her, America, in building up the base for a divine new world. In doing so, she will become doubly prosperous:

"Spiritual prosperity being added to the material, and both nourishing and serving the highest cause of a Divine New Creation." *Eternity's Breath, P.107, (1972),* Agni Press.

While America means speed, while it wants to run faster than the fastest, Sri Chinmoy felt that endurance was a quality that it initially lacked. In Sri Chinmoy's philosophy, stamina is equally as important as speed:

"If one has only speed, then one cannot ultimately succeed; we need endurance because the goal is quite far. Again, if one has only stamina and no speed, then it will take forever to reach the goal. Only if someone has both qualities will he be able to make very good progress in his spiritual life and achieve something really great in life." *The Outer Running and the Sri Chinmoy and Sudahota Carl Lewis, 1992, Manhattan Peace Concert. Inner Running, P160, (1984),* Agni Press

Sri Chinmoy gives examples of America's super-excellent long-distance runners such as Bill Rodgers, Frank Shorter and others, to demonstrate that America now feels that both speed and endurance are necessary, that it cares for both. He was also very fond of Jesse Owen, Carl Lewis and Bill Pearl, all three being among the elite of American sport, and embodying the qualities of discipline, dynamism, power and other aspects of the American dream.

To conclude, one sees that the idea of starting, not wasting time, of being consciously on the move and not hesitating once one knows where one's goal is, was of tremendous significance to Sri Chinmoy and to our Path. This America embodied to the highest, and as such was appealing to him. Many a time in my thirty years with my teacher and Mentor, Sri Chinmoy would get his students to sing songs dedicated to America or sing her own national anthem. Over the years, America's spirit of freedom, of power, of opulence and speed in a divine sense has been depicted in his student's many parades, dramas and plays.

In view of America's faithfulness to the prose below, one can see why it is a country with so much promise and why Sri Chinmoy chose to spend 43 years on her soil:

> "Once you feel that your goal is not where you are, that your goal is somewhere ahead of you, then you have to run. And if you run, eventually you are bound to reach your goal" *(Ibid. p. 161.)*

- Manatita, April 5ᵗʰ, 2010

CHAPTER NINE

Discipleship

".... True spirituality advocates both God-acceptance and life-acceptance. In true spirituality, the seeker first tries to realise God and then to manifest Him in and through his own life."

- Sri Chinmoy.
The Giver And The Receiver, (1987), Agni Press.

In the life of discipleship, the necessity of a Spiritual Master is paramount. Indeed Eastern philosophy teaches that for realisation of the Self, three things are necessary: The human birth, an intense yearning to realise God, and the living presence of the right Spiritual Teacher. One sees this loving relationship expressed in the lives of many men and women of God, among them Sri Daya Mata, Swami Vivekananda and Swami Brahmananda. Again in the *Gita,* we see Arjuna's doubts and dilemma being dispelled by his Guru, Lord Krishna, and in the courage which he took with him on the battlefield of Kurukshetra:

"Your words are wise, Arjuna, but your sorrow is for nothing. The truly wise mourn neither for the living nor for the dead." *Bhagavad Gita: The Song of God, P. 38, (1987),* Vedanta Press, California.

One can feel Sri Daya Mata's great love and devotion for her Master expressed in the following prose:

"Since I first set eyes on my Guru, Paramahansa Yogananda, almost forty years ago, it has been my joy to lay my heart, my mind, my soul, my mortal form, at the feet of God, in the hope that somehow he might use this life I have given to Him. Such soul satisfaction has filled these years; it is as though I am constantly drinking from the fountain of Love Divine. I can take no credit for this; it is the Guru's blessing, a blessing he bestows on all of us in the same way, if we but prepare ourselves to receive it." *Only Love, P16, (1976)*, Self-Realisation Fellowship, Los Angeles, California.

Sri Nisagadatta Maraharaj alludes to the significance of the Guru thus:

"To find a living Guru is a rare opportunity and a great responsibility." *I am That. P. 49; 305. (1986)*. Acorn Press.

Being at the feet of the Master can be described as a lifelong *Satsang* (spiritual practice). There is teaching, laughing, prayers and meditations, cheering, scolding, the personal aspect, and of course the imparting of Grace. Swami Vivekananda experienced this transmission, and expressed it most powerfully in the following paragraph:

"Two or three days before Sri Ramakrishna's passing away, he called me to his side, looked steadily at me, and went into Samadhi. Then I felt that a subtle force like an electric shock was entering my body! In a little while, I also lost outward consciousness, and sat motionless. How long I stayed in that condition, I do not remember. When consciousness returned, I found Sri Ramakrishna shedding tears. On questioning him, he answered me affectionately: 'Today, giving you my all, I have become a beggar. With this power, you are to do much work for the good of the world before you return.' *God Lived With Them, P37, (1997)*, Vedanta Society of St. Louis.

Of course this Grace is imperative in the life of the Disciple, for it not only cements his/her relationship with the Master, but enables the disciple to convey the Master's message to the world in a more meaningful and loving way. According to Sri Chinmoy, God's grace is like the rays of the sun, if one keeps one's heart's-door wide open, God's Light will enter into one's existence. This Grace or Compassion, work in the same or similar way only that Compassion is more intense:

"The same Grace, when it has tremendous intensity, is called Compassion. Water is everywhere, but when there is a torrential rain, you can say Compassion is descending. It is like a heavy downpour from above, with tremendous force." *God Is, P. 100*, Aum Publications, 1997.

"Grace is all in all." Says Papa Ramdas. *Thus Speaks Ramdas, Paragraph 63, (1984)*. Anandashram, India.

This Grace is God's love for the disciple. According to Sri Chinmoy, when it takes an intimate form it is called Compassion, the most powerful attribute, the most significant attribute of the Supreme. In the divine scheme of things, the Master's Compassion changes and transforms the disciple, and keeps him from making major mistakes in his spiritual life. Thus we see the necessity of a Master in *Discipleship,* as far as Grace is concerned.

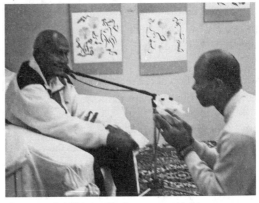

On Sri Chinmoy's Path, the life of the disciple is a great responsibility and a supreme blessing. Indeed the disciple is actually chosen. This was especially so in the lifetime of Sri Chinmoy:

Sri Chinmoy blessing me on my birthday.

"You have not chosen me, but I have chosen you"- Sri Chinmoy

"If you can feel that you are chosen by your Master to do his work, to fulfil the mission of the Supreme, your very realisation of this is your supreme gift to your Guru and to the Supreme."
A God-Lover's Earth-Heaven-Life, Part 3, (1974), Agni Press.

The disciple is consequently active in the outer world, manifesting Sri Chinmoy's message and vision to the world at large. To that extent, one could say that discipleship is rather like a sacrifice ... the throwing away of the old, that which does not satisfy the disciple or keeps him in darkness. Instead, replacing it with Light – the positive things that take him towards the Sun, and away from that void. The profound quote below expresses this:

"…. What one calls 'sacrifice', is really a constant self-giving based on one's awareness of universal oneness, and a constant heroic dynamism that enables one to conquer ignorance-sea in the battlefield of life, and transform it into a sea of Wisdom-light." *Behind the Curtain of Eternity, P. 26, (2008),* Aum Publications.

It is important to mention that the word 'disciple', as used by Sri Chinmoy for his students, took on a more personal and committed approach than the word 'seeker' as it is generally used. The latter mostly signifies someone with an interest in the spiritual life, but not necessarily having a spiritual Mentor. Seekers are often sincere, but free to visit different Paths. They are by nature enquiring, but may or may not be generally committed to a single Path and the consecrated life.

Again, Sri Chinmoy also used the word in the sense that we are all seekers, paving our way on the road to God-realisation and the journey of self-transcendence. Indeed it seems that the real seeker, the genuine seeker, can be as devotional and surrendered as the disciple himself, if not more so. However, while the seeker is not necessarily a disciple, the disciple is always a seeker. The profundity of the seeker is expressed thus:

"A seeker's life is his blossoming love. A seeker's blossoming love is his illuming light. A seeker's life becomes the many and the one. A seeker's life becomes the one and the many. A seeker's life is at once dependent and independent. His is the life boundlessly dependent on God. His is the life sleeplessly independent of ignorance. A seeker has belief, he has faith, he has conviction, he has realisation. God does everything; this is his spotless faith. God is all love. This is his peerless conviction. God is His own Eternity's Silence, God is His own Infinity's Sound, and God is His own Immortality's satisfaction: This is his ageless realisation." Sri Chinmoy continues:

"A true seeker's life and his gratitude-heart are always inseparable. By virtue of his gratitude-heart, he sees the invisible, he feels the unimaginable, and he achieves the impossible. He sees the invisible perfection within and without him. He feels the unimaginable satisfaction in his entire being. He achieves the impossible: God's God-heights and God's God-depths. A seeker's life embodies two supreme realities: His conscious, constant and soulful self-giving prayer and his loving, devoted and unreserved God-becoming meditation" *Oneness of the Eastern Heart and the Western Mind, Vol. 3, P. 149. (2004),* Agni Press.

Nevertheless, the relationship between Master and disciple was sometimes described by Sri Chinmoy as of a private tutor and his student, indeed even more than a motherly-fatherly one. Here, the Supreme is the disciple's only Friend. Such a relationship involves guidance, advocacy, encouragement, responsibility, acceptance, grace and the love that comes with realisation of the Self. For the disciple's part, it requires faith, obedience, acceptance, devotion, gratitude, service, love and aspiration amongst many other qualities. As asserted by Sri Chinmoy, in the relationship between Master and disciple, both are needed to fulfil each other:

"The Spiritual Master is a flower, And his instruments are the petals.
Without the flower, there can be no petals.
Again, if the petals have fallen away,
Who will appreciate the flower?"

Behind the Curtain of Eternity, P. 48, (2008), Aum Publications.

According to Sri Chinmoy, discipleship requires acceptance by the Master, who makes a promise to the Supreme and to the Soul of the individual seeker, that he, the Master, is eternally responsible for that Soul. Such acceptance has to be mutual, says Sri Chinmoy, with an inner feeling from the disciple that the Master has accepted him, not only in one incarnation, but also in future incarnations. Sri Chinmoy also indicates that he takes on the disciple's imperfections, constantly trying to bring to the fore the inner divinity of the disciple from deep within the disciple's heart. Having awakened the divine child, he tells the Soul:

"You will look after the other members of the family – the physical, the mind and the vital – and take care of them. They are making mistakes constantly, now give them new life, new meaning, new purpose." *The Master and the Disciple, P. 8, (1985).* Agni Press.

Sri Chinmoy taught that:

"The most important thing a Spiritual Master does for his spiritual children is to make them consciously aware of something vast and infinite within themselves, which is nothing other than God Himself" *(Ibid. p. 8).*

In Sri Chinmoy's teaching, the Master is a necessary guide. This enables the seeker to avoid being slow and uncertain in his *Sadhana*, as well as staving off confusion and doubts along the way. Additionally, the Master is there to encourage and inspire the disciple in his life of spiritual pursuit and love for God. With the Master-disciple relationship, initiation is paramount:

"At the time of initiation, the Master actually takes on the disciple's teeming imperfections, both from the present incarnation, and from past incarnations." *(Ibid. p.12).* How is this initiation done? Sri Chinmoy explains:

"When the Master initiates someone, he gives that person a portion of his life-breath. At the time of initiation, the Guru makes a solemn promise to the individual seeker and to the Supreme that he will do his best to help the seeker in his spiritual life, that he will offer his heart and soul to take the disciple, into the highest region of the beyond." *(Ibid. p. 11).*

According to Sri Chinmoy, initiation can be performed in various ways: through meditation, through sleeping and waking, through the eyes, or physically touching the person, or in a psychic way. It can also be done by occult processes or in a dream. With initiation, the disciple is accepted unreservedly and unconditionally. Consequently, even if the disciple leaves the Master's Path, he is still bound to help him because of the promise he, the Master, has made to the Supreme. What is the purpose of initiation?

"The main purpose of initiation is to bring the Soul to the fore. If there is no initiation, the purification of the body, vital, mind and heart can never be complete. If there is no initiation, then the highest goal can never be realised." *(Ibid).*

Interestingly enough, initiation is not something that disciples discuss much on Sri Chinmoy's Path. I myself have not knowingly thought about it in any great detail. One can say, perhaps, that the writings of the Master right from the start, spoke with such authority that I was saturated in its love.

Again, that loving and compassionate smile, that illumining gaze, is more than enough to dispel my doubt for an entire period of discipleship. Finally, there is that 'inner connection,' that sweet feeling or deep inner thrill that one experiences with or without the Master's physical Presence, and the intuitive feel that the Master is here for eternity, is more than adequate for the true disciple.

Sri Chinmoy speaks of an actual flowering of initiation the moment the disciple's entire life is dedicated to God. According to Sri Chinmoy, as the disciple's divinity comes to the fore, he feels that he and his Guru have become totally one, and that he has no existence without his Guru. Consequently, he learns that only by fulfilling the Supreme first, can he fulfil the rest of the world.

For the disciple's part, what's required is that he stays in the Master's boat, and in the inmost recesses of the Master's heart, existing only for the fulfilment of his will. His life now has no other purpose. Again the Master plays his part by taking the ignorance and impurity from the disciple, carrying them faithfully and devotedly to the Supreme. In this way, they fulfil each other. *(Ibid. p. 8).*

For discipleship with the Master, one understands it to be paramount to have a very loving and close relationship with the Master, the disciple relying on him for his realisation, and the Master utilising the disciple for the manifestation of God's light here on Earth. In this way, both complement each other. According to Sri Chinmoy, the Master needs disciples as they are an expression of his own consciousness. When the Master gets the command from the Highest to do something on Earth, then he has to try to find those who are going to be part and parcel of his consciousness to help him fulfil that command.

Sri Chinmoy spoke of the disciple's problems as his very own, and the disciple understood that his Guru would often take these problems, working them out on his own body. He spoke of Grace or the Supreme as having the last say, not fate or *Karma*, and that fate can be changed by an unchanging will, a life of dedication to the Supreme, the Master's will or God Itself, operating in and through the disciple. *(Ibid. p. 47).*

Sri Chinmoy referred to what he called 'emanations', as 'a ray from my inner sun.' They act as messengers to inform the Master, of the disciple's physical and psychic difficulties:-

"In those whom I consider to be my true disciples, I put a spiritual spark of my own soul. My soul is like the sun. The day I make the inner promise to a disciple and accept him as my very own, I put a ray from my inner sun inside him. You can call it an emanation; it need not be an emanation; in some cases there are more than one emanations … if something very serious or striking happens, the emanations will tell me." *Behind the Curtain of Eternity, pp.103 - 5, (2008).* Aum Publications.

In Sri Chinmoy's philosophy, the disciple is expected to stay on one Path. While freely admitting that there are other Paths, it is important not to change so as to accelerate one's progress. Changing Path's, to Sri Chinmoy, was like changing lanes on a motorway, or crossing the ocean in a raft. He saw it as being very dangerous. *The Master and the Disciple, P. 1, (1985).* Agni Press

"A teacher is like a boat," he would say, "If you are in one boat, you are safe. But if you keep one leg in one boat and another leg in another boat, then you will just fall into the sea of ignorance." *(Ibid. p. 28).*

"The goal is one, but Paths are many, you cannot constantly change Paths and hope to make the same speed. The seeker has to be wise, careful and discriminating." *(Ibid).*

"Once you choose a Master, you have to stick to his Path with total dedication and surrender. For you can only travel on one road at a time." *(Ibid. pp. 14-15).*

In Sri Chinmoy's teachings, the Master communicates with the souls of his disciples on a daily basis, feeding them with light, peace and bliss:-

".... every day the Master is telling the Souls how they can please the Supreme, and the Souls are bringing the message to the disciple's conscious mind. Then the disciples either accept or reject the message." *(Ibid. p. 56).*

And again:

"He will simply meditate on you and inwardly teach you how to meditate. Your soul will enter into his soul and learn from his soul." *God Is. P. 31, (1997).* Aum Publications.

Sri Chinmoy spoke of many classes of disciples, sometimes three, seven, eight or even nine classes. Again, he also spoke of followers, admirers, well-wishers and friends. Some of them, while not considered to be disciples by his students, were nevertheless, close to or had access to him physically in his lifetime. *(The Master and the Disciple, P 60, (1985), Agni Press).*

At this point it is worth mentioning that in the life of the disciple, commitment and devotion to God is necessary. This is reflected by a steady daily discipline of prayer and meditation, especially in the early hours of the morning. Again this is to be done at a time practically reasonable for the disciple in keeping with the nature of his work, while at the same time harmonising with nature's peace and silence. Sri Chinmoy has recommended 6.a.m. and again at nights, prior to retiring to sleep. A sincere and dedicated approach to a change in lifestyle, soulful self-giving, and in living a more wholesome life, was also one of the recommendations of Sri Chinmoy.

To conclude, one sees that ultimately the seeker needs the Master for his realisation, and that the Master needs him for manifestation. We have seen also that discipleship is paramount. Again there has to be total consecration to the Supreme – an acceptance of the Master and a flowering of the inner divinity through initiation. The Master then becomes rather like a gardener, with the flowers in the garden serving to enhance the Master's cause. For this to take place, compassion and gratitude are always there; encouragement and justice also, to expedite the disciple's progress in his life's purpose of unconditional surrender to God and the evolution of humanity through a life of constant service to God and man.

This relationship continues after the Guru leaves the body, with the Master supporting and guiding the disciple from the inner planes. On the disciple's part, his life of consecration and devotion to God continues, with an unshakable faith that his Guru is guiding him, even though no longer present in the physical body.

Kuching, Malaysia, 31th December, 2008.

CHAPTER TEN

The True Seeker
(Excerpts from Sri Chinmoy's Writings)

"…A true seeker is he who continually wants to grow, glow and flow in the heart of the Absolute Supreme. He loves God and serves God not because God is all powerful, but because God is all goodness… He loves God because he knows that without God, he does not exist. He serves God because he feels that without him, God does not exist."

"At every moment, a true seeker has to love God and serve God with a pure heart and a clear mind. A heart of purity and a mind of clarity each seeker must possess in order to accelerate his inner progress and outer success."

"A true seeker offers to God what he has and what he is. What he has is ignorance. What he is is a gratitude-heart. When he offers his gratitude-heart, he becomes a chosen instrument of the Supreme. A chosen instrument at times pleases God in his own way; at other times he pleases God in God's own Way. There comes a time when the chosen instrument is transformed into an unconditionally surrendered instrument. An unconditionally surrendered instrument of God pleases God at every moment in God's own way…"

" .. This expresses a real acceptance of life, not a rejection of life. True spirituality is the acceptance of earth-life. A tree seeker is he who accepts life, transcends life and perfects life, so that the earth-life can become a conscious instrument of God … "

"..True spirituality advocates both God-acceptance and life-acceptance. In true spirituality, the seeker first tries to realise God, and then to manifest Him in and through his own life." *The Oneness Of The Eastern Heart And The Western Mind, Part 1, Pages 96+97. October (2003),* Agni Press

"The seeker is he who has freed himself from the desire-world, from the meshes of ignorance. He wants only the truth and nothing else…." …A true seeker is he who sees God not only in the highest plane of consciousness, but also in the lowest, unlit plane of consciousness The seeker enters into the lowest in order to bring down the Reality-Light of the Highest so that he can transform the lowest into the Highest. The seeker accepts earth as a reality, and in this reality, through this reality, the seeker knows that God-vision manifests itself." *(Ibid. p. 99).*

"A true seeker is he who constantly prays to God and yet consciously remains unconscious of his prayer. A true seeker is he who sleeplessly meditates on God and yet deliberately remains unconscious of his meditation. A true seeker is he who soulfully loves the world and yet easily remains unconscious of his love. A true seeker is he who devotedly serves the world and yet surprisingly remains unconscious of his service."

"God has a special liking for a true seeker because of his sincerity-life. God has a special love for a true seeker because of his purity-heart. A true seeker has a special liking for God, not because God gives him infinitely more than he needs, but because God gives him his Infinity's Compassion. A true seeker has a special love for God, not because God gives him infinitely more than he deserves, but because God is his Eternity's Forgiveness" *The Oneness Of The Eastern Heart And The Western Mind, Part Two, P 149, (2004).* Agni Press.

"A seekers' life is his blossoming love. A seeker's blossoming love is his illumining light."

"A seeker's life becomes the many and the One. A seeker's love becomes the One and the many."

"A seeker's life is at once dependent and independent. His is the life boundlessly dependent on God. His is the life sleeplessly independent of ignorance."

"A seeker has belief, he has faith, he has conviction, he has realisation. God does everything: This is his faultless belief. God is everything: this is his spotless faith. God is all love: This is his peerless conviction. God is His own Eternity's Silence, God is His own Infinity's Sound, and God is His own Immortality's Satisfaction: this is his ageless realisation."

"A true seeker's life and his gratitude-heart are always inseparable. By virtue of his gratitude-heart he sees the invisible, he feels the unimaginable, and he achieves the impossible. He sees the invisible perfection within and without him. He feels the unimaginable satisfaction in his entire being. He achieves the impossible: God's God-Heights and God's God-Depths."

"A seeker's life embodies two supreme realities: his conscious, constant and soulful self-giving prayer and his loving, devoted and unreserved God-becoming meditation." *(Ibid. p. 153).*

"… A seeker has to be like a tree. A tree always serves. From the root of the tree right up to the topmost bough, it is all sacrifice. The seed, the branches, the leaves, and the fruit – everything in the tree is constantly ready to serve. When a tree serves us, we do not feel that the tree is inferior to us in any way. On the contrary, we offer our gratitude to the tree. The nobility of the tree, and the generosity of the tree, receive our gratitude."

"…. The life of a seeker is the life of a server, and the life of a server is the life of a liberator of aspiring humanity." *The Oneness Of The Eastern Heart And The Western Mind, P 1, 81, (2003)*. Agni Press.

- Manatita January, 2009.

CHAPTER ELEVEN

Love, Devotion and Surrender: A Glimpse into the Sunlit Path of Sri Chinmoy

"....Always remember the Golden Shore. Our eternal Goal is the Golden Shore. Always feel that there is a shore and that there is a boat. The boat is the symbol of the journey. We arrive there to help humanity come to their goal."

-Sri Chinmoy.

The Golden Boat. Sri Chinmoy Centre Emblem painted by Sri Chinmoy.

On God First

My Lord Beloved Supreme
"My Lord beloved Supreme, with every breath of my heart,
I enter into Your heart, to love You only, in Your own way.
My Lord Beloved Supreme, with every breath of my heart,
I sit at Your feet, to need You only, in Your own way.
My Lord Beloved Supreme, with every breath of my heart,
I look at Your eye, to fulfil You only, in Your own way"
A Day In The Life Of A Sri Chinmoy Disciple, P. 10, (April 2008). Agni Press.

Since I am going to be presenting the argument that God comes first, perhaps I should begin with the dear and loving term, 'Supreme', that Sri Chinmoy uses for God and to quote his reasons. This I will now do by allowing Sri Chinmoy to speak for himself:

"All religious faiths have the same God but they address Him differently. A man will be called 'Father' by one person, 'Brother' by another and 'Uncle' by another. Then when that person goes to the office, he is called by his surname.

Sri Chinmoy in Meditation

When he mixes with his friends, they will call him by his given name. He is the same person but he is addressed in different ways, according to one's connection with him. Similarly, God is also addressed in various ways, according to one's sweetest, most affectionate feeling.

Instead of using the word 'God', I use the word 'Supreme' most of the time. I ask my disciples to do the same, for I feel it gives us a more intimate connection with Him. Of course, only Spiritual Masters can know the difference between these highest spiritual Realities. Many people may ask me, "Why do you have to separate 'God' and the 'Supreme'? They are just synonyms." But although God and the Supreme are one, there is a subtle distinction between the two. The Highest Supreme is different from what we call God.

When we speak of God-realisation, here 'God,' is synonymous with the Supreme. But usually when we say 'God', we feel that He embodies a height which is static. He is like a mountain that is high, but flat. When we use the term 'God', we feel that He has reached His Height and stopped. He does not have a constantly evolving Consciousness; He is something finished, a finished product. But when we say

> 'Supreme', we are speaking of the Supreme Lord who not only reaches the Absolute Highest, but all the time goes beyond, beyond, and transcends the Beyond. There is a constant upward movement." *The Vision of God's Dawn, (1974)*, Agni Press.

Sri Chinmoy is not different from God-Men such as The Christ, The Buddha, Lord Krishna and others, in stating quite categorically that God must come first. Indeed, Sri Chinmoy suggests that we depend on Him for every little thought and action, at every second, in order to feel that we need Him alone. The secret of the Highest Truth, according to Sri Chinmoy, is not to long for anything except God, the Supreme Light.

This is a message we see also in the teachings of Jesus, the Christ:

"But seek ye first the kingdom of God, and His righteousness; and all these things shall be added unto you. Take therefore no thought for the morrow: for the morrow shall take thought for the things of itself. Sufficient unto the day is the evil thereof" *The Holy Bible. King James Version. Matthew Chpt. 6, verses 33 -34.*

Again Jesus tells us that there is none good but God, and that he can of his own self do nothing. (*The Holy Bible. King James Version. John 5:30*).

He makes frequent references to 'The Father' and goes off into the wilderness to pray to Him. His immortal prayer to mankind begins with, "Our Father." He then goes on to glorify Him with 'Hallowed be Thy name ...' and 'Thy will be done on earth as it is in heaven' *The Holy Bible: King James Version. Matthew Chpt. 6, verse 9-10.*

Sri Krishna uses a different approach, as, like all Divine Incarnations, he alternates between the human and the divine as the occasion demands. That is to say, he sometimes speaks like Brahman (God), and at other times he refers to Brahman. Here are some examples:

"Devote your whole mind to Me, and practice Yoga. Take Me for your only refuge" "That Yogi sees Me in all things and all things within Me. He never loses sight of Me, nor I of Him. He is established in union with Me, and worships Me devoutly in all beings"

"Be absorbed in Me. Lodge your mind in Me: Thus you shall dwell in Me." Sri Krishna continues in a most devotional vein:

"Mentally resign all your actions to Me. Regard me as your Dearest loved One. Know Me to be your only refuge. Be united always in heart and consciousness with Me."

"Give Me your whole heart. Love and adore Me. Worship Me always. Bow to Me only, and you shall find Me." Finally, he seeks to comfort Arjuna for taking refuge in him:

"Lay down all duties in Me, your refuge. Fear no longer, for I will save you from sin and from bondage." *Bhagavad Gita: The Song of God, P. 80, 86,162, 163. (1987)* Trans. by C. Isherwood; Swami Prabhavananda. Vedanta Press, California.

Sri Chinmoy spoke like that when he encouraged us to feel that our breath was coming from and entering into his Heart, and that our entire existence was under his loving care. In a manner of speaking, we needed to have faith and to keep our mind and heart on him at all times. However, he always stressed that the Supreme was the only Doer, and to feel that God, the Supreme, was responsible for all our activities.

By dedicating all our actions to God, we would get, he says, infinite capacity, and the hostile forces would be automatically conquered. By offering everything to him, he would place them at the feet of the Supreme. Every sincere Master, Sri Chinmoy taught, is like a bridge in the disciple's life, and should be always first. This is covered in the Chapter on *Discipleship* (Chapter nine), and elsewhere in Sri Chinmoy's writing.

In Sri Chinmoy's philosophy, God is not only first, but second and last. God is all in all. It is by going to the Source first, that one gets everything else. As such in whatever way we as disciples manifest the Supreme, it is always with that devotional bent and with God in mind. Here are a couple of quotations from my beloved Teacher:

"...the essence, the quintessence of society is God, so spiritual people try
to enter into the essence first" ... *The Oneness Of The Eastern Heart And The
Western Mind, Part 1, (2003),* Agni Press.

".. First things first, mean that God should come first in our life – not
only in our inner life, but also in our daily multifarious activities. It means that
God is to be loved first and foremost, both as the Deity and as all human
beings"

" .. He is our success. He is our failure, He is the Doer and He is the
action. If we can see God's presence in each action, then see the action itself
as God, and later the result – success or failure – as God, and finally the Doer
Himself as God, then all our problems are over" *(Ibid. pp. 71,163,303.)*

Sri Chinmoy continues in very much the same vein in the next two
examples:

"Love your family much. This is your great duty. Love mankind more. This
is your greater duty. Love God most. This is your greatest duty, the Duty
Supreme." *(Ibid. Pt 2, p.18, (2004).*

That love of God was and is always emphasised in our service. In the
morning through prayer, before we undertake anything in our lives such as
eating, working, and certainly in major undertakings. This includes driving,
flying and other endeavours. We are asked to, and always try to remember the
Supreme first. I have never seen Sri Chinmoy dedicate anything without
bowing to the Supreme, or offering his folded hands or paying homage to
God in others, and this same thread runs throughout his 1600 books.

"You are spiritual; that means God comes first in your life. You are
spiritual; that means that God is the only reality in your life. You are spiritual;
that means that God is your life's constant voice" *(Ibid. Vol.3, p.30, (2004).*

It is essentially important and of tremendous significance to remember,
and indeed to feel that one is simply an instrument in the hands of Something
Higher. This approach aids significantly in avoiding the trappings of the *ego*
and ensuring a greater sense of humility. Above all, one should engage in a
loving and infinite relationship with God. That is why I am dwelling on this
'God first' aspect so early in this Chapter. I have placed Sri Chinmoy's sacred
Morning Prayer, *My Lord Beloved Supreme,* right at the beginning of this Chapter,
just to emphasise this. Speaking of this prayer, Sri Chinmoy tells us:

"This prayer embodies the meaning of our Path. We did not create this prayer, but God created it so He could teach us how to pray to Him. *A Day in the Life of a Sri Chinmoy Disciple,* Lake Atitlan, Guatemala, December 12th, 1997.

So we see here that God is our true possession, our eternal possession; our only possession is our love of God. The Supreme has to come first in everything, and that the Master, being our Bridge to the Supreme, is more intimate to us than our life activities. There can be no happiness in life unless we make God happy. I will now end the first part of this Chapter with a most exquisite quote from Guru Sri Chinmoy:

"... There are some aspirants who do not want anything from God except God Himself. They feel that if they get God they get everything. They are like hungry children in a garden where there is a tree laden with the most delicious mangoes. They know that if they can please the owner of the tree, they will get all the mangoes on the tree. Here God is the owner of the tree, and at the same time He is the tree. When we please Him, He satisfies our hunger for infinite Light, Peace and Bliss. If the aspirants are wise, they know that the moment they please God, they get everything from Him"- *The Oneness of the Eastern Heart and the Western Mind, Vol2, P 77 (2004),* Agni Press.

On God Itself

We have spent some time talking about and putting God first. Still, who or what is God? What are our concepts of It? This is what some of my friends will call 'a transcendental question.' Certainly all the God-Men – in my experience – say that this experience is beyond words. So how can we know God? Well, a certain conviction, a certain and inner unshakable Faith in things unseen or seen is necessary. But who tells us this? There is a story of a Spiritual Master from the East who said that words were not necessary. "But Master", said one devotee. "Why then do you use words?

"Only to take you to the point where you realise that words are not necessary", said the Master. Certainly Sri Chinmoy has made an unparalleled use of written words, to the tune of nearly 1600 books!

Sri Guru Nanak Dev, the first Sikh Guru, in the sacred text Japji Sahib, says that it is through words that the word of God is conveyed to us. It is through words that His praises are sung; it is through words that we become familiar with His attributes and become followers of His virtues. Again, it is through words that languages are spoken and written. *Essence of Japji Sahib, P43 – 44. April (2004)* Delux printers, Acton, UK.

Perhaps God can best be said to be Absolute. (Existence, Consciousness and Bliss) Few seem to argue with this idea.

Before I give you some of Sri Chinmoy's definitions, let us just say for convenience sake that at the core of everything in the phenomenal world is a Divine Ground – a Perennial Entity from which all things spring, live and have their Being, and without which there would be no existence. Man and this Existence are essentially one, and so he has only one true purpose, that of becoming one with this Existence, enriching his experiences along the way. Different Paths call it by different names. The reader may wish to read Aldous Huxley, in his introduction to the *Bhagavad Gita, 4th Edit*, (1987), by C. Isherwood and Swami Phabhavananda, where he describes this concept very beautifully.

Sri Chinmoy says that everyone's definition of God is correct in its own way. It is given according to one's understanding, capacity, inner awakening or illumination. He continues to tell us that while some may say that God is Light, others say that He is Consciousness. Still others will say that He is Power, and a fourth that He is a personal Being and so forth. Here are some of Sri Chinmoy's definitions:

Sri Chinmoy in contemplation

"According to my realisations, my personal definition of God is love. He is dearest to me because in Him I see infinite Love. I see that He is both the Eternal Lover and the Eternal Beloved. Inside the heart of the individual seeker, before the seeker realises the Highest, God is the Lover. But to that very same seeker who is aspiring for the Highest, God is the Beloved Himself. Eventually the Lover and the Beloved become totally one. Man and God are eternally one. Man is God yet to be realised fully, consciously and integrally; God is man yet to be manifested totally on Earth" *The Inner Journey, P 46 – 47*, (1977), Agni Press.

Or this poetic and inspiring definition:

"When I think that the Flute and the Flautist are two different things, I think of myself as God's servant and Him as my Master. When I feel that the Flute has a part of His Master's consciousness, I feel that I am God's child and He is my Father. Finally, when I realise that the Flute and the Flautist are but one, the Flautist appears as the Spirit and I as its creative force" *Yoga and the Spiritual Life, P 2, (1977)*, Agni Press.

Playing flute outside Kyoto Station, Japan, 1992.

Purpose of Life

What is the purpose of life? Why are we here? The great Soul Mahapurush Swami Shivananda, a disciple of Sri Ramakrishna cautions us:

" ... You must be ever watchful about the goal; you must never forget the aim of life." *For Seekers of God, 4th Edit.* (1975) Union Press, India. (Back cover)

Sri Chinmoy, like all God-men, made beautiful use of imagery, metaphors and analogies. He often spoke of a 'Golden Shore'. There is a boat and a Boatman at the helm. In that boat are disciples and He, the Master, is the Captain at the helm. The Supreme, or the Master, to the disciple, is the one that knows the way and will take the disciple to the goal. Here one can be active such as rowing or even sleeping. All that is required is simply to remain in that boat and the Boatman – the Guru – will take us to the Golden Shore. Indeed this Golden Boat is the emblem of Sri Chinmoy's Path. Once we get to this Golden Shore, then the role of the Boatman is over. Again, Guruji describes life's purpose in a most profound and illumining way:

> "Your soul has a special mission. Your soul is supremely conscious of it. Maya, illusion or forgetfulness, makes you feel that you are finite, weak and helpless. This is not true. You are not the body. You are not the senses. You are not the mind. These are all limited. You are the Soul, which is unlimited. Your soul is infinitely powerful. Your soul defies all time and space. Can you ever realise your soul? Can you be fully conscious of your soul and be one with it? Certainly you can. For in fact you are nothing other than the Soul …. Your special mission – which is the fulfilment of your divinity – is not outside you but within you. Search within. Meditate within. You will discover your mission" *Yoga and The Spiritual Life, P 31-33*, (1977), Agni Press.

I would now look at the Goal of life from a three-fold aspect, based on my own understanding of Sri Chinmoy's teachings. First there is God-realisation (Self- realisation), a state of man's total, conscious, constant and inseparable oneness with God, the Supreme. Sri Chinmoy describes it as irreversible. Then there is Self- transcendence – I have dedicated Chapter 7 to it. Finally there is the sweetest of the sweet: Surrender. Here they are as I see them:

1. God-realisation
2. Self-transcendence
3. Total and unconditional Surrender to the Will of the Supreme.

Here are some paragraphs expressing the depth and breadth of realisation:

> **Realisation:** *"Realisation* is our conscious, constant and inseparable universal oneness" says Sri Chinmoy.

> " … Realisation is the perfection of our inner nature, and our conscious surrender to God's cosmic will. At every moment, a realised soul feels His conscious and constant oneness with the Will of the Absolute Supreme" *The*

Oneness of The Eastern Heart and the Western Mind, Part One, P171, 100. (2003) Agni Press.

"… when you are God-realised, you consciously know what God is, what He looks like, what He wills. When you achieve Self-realisation, you remain in God's consciousness and speak to God face to face. You see God both in the finite and in the infinite. You see God as both personal and impersonal … there can be no ignorance. So you can speak to God more clearly, more intimately, more openly than to a human being." Finally:

> "God-realisation is self-discovery in the highest sense of the term – the conscious realisation of your oneness with God. As long as you remain in ignorance, you will feel that God is somebody else who has infinite power, whereas you are the feeblest person on Earth. But the moment you realise God, you come to know that you and God are absolutely one in both the inner and the outer life. God-realisation means your realisation with your own Highest Self. When you can identify with your Highest Self and remain in that consciousness forever, when you can reveal and manifest it at your own command, at that time you will know that you have realised God. *The Master and the Disciple, P35, (1985),* Agni Press.

Self-transcendence: Next is *Self-transcendence* - going beyond, beyond, into the ever-transcending beyond. (Covered in Chapter 7). Sri Chinmoy says that the message of Self-transcendence is the highest message that God has handed down to mankind. Its only aim is progress, by competing, not with others, but with ourselves:

> "Self-transcendence gives us joy in boundless measure. When we transcend ourselves, we do not compete with others. We do not compete with the rest of the world, but at every moment we compete with ourselves." *The Vision-sky of California, (1980),* Agni Press.

Surrender: Finally, we come to my favourite: *Surrender.* This is what My Guru Sri Chinmoy has to say in this respect:

> "An aspirant has to know his Goal. If his Goal is God-realisation, he can start with that in mind. But the Ultimate Goal is unconditional surrender to God's will. When God sees that His child, His most devoted child, has made this unconditional surrender – not for a second, not for a day or a year, but for a whole lifetime, for all incarnations to come, for all Eternity – then alone God embraces His dearest, His sweetest, His most devoted

child. When that embrace takes place, man changes into God himself." *The Oneness Of The Eastern Heart And The Western Mind, Vol Two, P. 77,* (2004), Agni Press.

Permit me to indulge finally, with a very powerful and sublime example of *Surrender* from the same page as above:

"On the strength of his sincere aspiration, a true seeker says, 'O God, if you feel that I should have Your vision, if you feel that You want to fulfil yourself in me and through me, if You feel that You can utilise me as Your instrument, I am at Your service. If You want me to stand before You, I shall come and stand. If You want to stand before me, I shall be equally happy. If you do not want either, but want somebody else to stand before You, I shall still be happy.' This is what we call Surrender. This is the ultimate Surrender." *The Oneness of The Eastern Heart And The Western Mind, Vol Two, P. 77,* (2004), Agni Press.

Love, Devotion and Surrender

"Love is sweet, devotion is sweeter, surrender is sweetest.

Love is sweet. I have felt this truth in my mother's spontaneous love for me.

Devotion is sweeter. I have discovered this truth in my mother's pure devotion towards the perfection of my life.

Surrender is the sweetest. I have realized this truth in my mother's constant surrender towards the fulfillment of my joy.

Again, love is mighty, devotion is mightier, surrender is the mightiest.

Love is mighty. This truth I feel when I look at my father's face.

Devotion is mightier. This truth I discover when I sit at the feet of my father.

Surrender is the mightiest. This truth I realize when I live in the breath of my father's will" *My Rose Petals, Part1, (1971),* Agni Press.

Love: Having established a sense of the priority given to the Source and life's purpose, perhaps we can now look more closely at Sri Chinmoy's philosophy: the Sunlit Path, the Path of the Heart. I begin with Love. Here love plays a supremely significant role:

> "Love is the root; love is the foundation of our Path. We feel that God is dearer to us not because He is omniscient, omnipresent and omnipotent, but just because He is all love." *The Oneness of The Eastern Heart And The Western Mind, Part One, P. 173, (2003)*, Agni Press.

"The highest spiritual force is love. There can be no force as effective as love. Love on the physical plane binds and limits us. It is a song of possession and attachment. But spiritual love expands and liberates us. It is a song of illumination and liberation for ourselves and others" *(Ibid. p. 408)*.

"When the heart comes to the fore, immediately we feel tremendous joy, relief and satisfaction. We feel that God is ours. When we use our heart, we claim God as our very own on the strength of our oneness. When we use the heart, there is no obstacle which cannot be surmounted. As a child has established his oneness with the mother, even so we can also establish our oneness with God on the strength of our spontaneous love for Him" *Canada Aspires, Canada Receives, Canada Achieves Part 2,* (1974). Agni Press,

"A nation can flourish when it sees no difference between the Creator and the Creation, when it loves the world not for what the world will give in return, but love for its own sake. Selfless love, true love never ends, never fails. Love is its own immediate reward." *The Life of Sri Chinmoy, Part Two, P. 49, (1984)*, Agni Press.

How Sri Chinmoy showed us this fatherly love and much more! He was compassionate, attentive, caring and loving; he would instruct and advise us collectively or individually, as well as scold us for our own benefit when we did wrong. He gave us so much of his time when we were around him! Whether it was in New York or in some country around the world, we always had a small or large gathering with him. Here he would chat, laugh, tell jokes or bring out the best in us in other ways. He was like a private tutor, taking interest in every one of his pupils and teaching us according to our capacity and receptivity.

"The end of all inner teaching is love', he once said, 'the divine love, not human love..... Divine love is expansion, enlargement, the feeling of one's true oneness." *My Rose Petals, P. 42, 43, (European Talks),* 1970) Sri Chinmoy Centre, Inc.

"Love radiates the life of harmony, brightens the joy of consciousness and sharpens the sword of intuition. Love is also ready to meet man's every soulful demand. Love conquers all that is unlike God. It is, indeed, supreme over all." *Songs Of The Soul, P. 35, (1971),* Agni Press.

Below, to my mind, is one of Sri Chinmoy's most intimate pieces of writing, where this unparalleled love is demonstrated for us:

"My spiritual children,
if I have love, if I have compassion, If I have light, if I have power,
If I have delight,
Then it is all for you, all for you, all for you.
O my sweet children,
it is with you, for you and in you that I exist here on earth"

Anniversary Message of 13 April 1967. *Sri Chinmoy, My* Consulate Years, *P.140. ,*(1996), Agni Press / Aum Publications, Jamaica, NY Finally, Sri

Chinmoy covers Love, Devotion and Surrender thus:

"... Love is self-expansion. Divine love expands and enlarges itself. Devotion is the intensity in love, and Surrender is the fulfilment of love." *The Oneness Of The Eastern Heart And The Western Mind, Part One, P. 367,* (2003), Agni Press.

It is important to realise that Sri Chinmoy is talking about the love that frees and not the love that binds. According to him, the love that illumines, the love that unites the length and breadth of the world, that is the love that God is bringing to the fore in the inner world. This message we see in biblical teachings thus:

"God is love, and he that dwelleth in love dwelleth in God and God in him"

"He that loveth not knoweth not God, for God is love" *The Holy Bible: King James Version. 1 John 4:8, 16.*

Devotion: Our Master taught that if one loves one's father, naturally one would want to serve him. If we can offer that love and more to God the Supreme Father, then like a magnet, it pulls God towards us. Constant, sleepless and breathless devotion is necessary to avoid dry periods and maintain sweetness in life. Devotion, according to Sri Chinmoy, is blessedness itself, the one-pointed dedication to the Supreme in the Master, to God Itself.

I can say that our devotion was tested in many ways. One simple and cute way which many of us remember with much love, is that the Master rarely seemed to pay any attention to the elements.

So sometimes it would rain in the middle of a performance, and all 1400 – 1500 of us would just continue without the slightest budge. Occasionally, our Guru would ask us to get an umbrella, but even then some people would rather be soaked just sitting in the presence of the Master. I have never known anyone to get sick as a result, and, on the contrary, disciples would always go away chatting and happy post such an event. Of the special guests, who were sometimes present and well shaded, Guru once said that their being there helped as they were benefitted by being able to see the devotion in his disciples. Here are some more eloquent expressions of devotion:

> "Devotion is the intensification of the seekers dedication to the Supreme Cause. His whole life becomes an altar of intensification. Everything that he does, he does with an intensification of his dedicated, devoted, unreserved and surrendered heart." *The Oneness of the Eastern Heart and the Western Mind, Vol Three, P 122, (2004)* Agni Press.

And finally, as always, a lofty quote from Sri Chinmoy:

> "To serve, and never be tired is Love. To learn and never be filled is Devotion. To offer and never to end, is Surrender. Love is man's reality. Devotion is man's divinity, and Surrender is man's immortality" *AUM: The Message of Sri Chinmoy, Vol V1, No 12, P 11,* (1971) Aum Press.

Surrender: The third aspect of Guru's philosophy I covered earlier on. Surrender is our conscious oneness with God's Will. It is the highest rung of the spiritual ladder and through my own experiences, I feel that it is not at all easy to achieve. Nevertheless, our Guru lived that life to show us the endless possibilities, if only we dare to believe and have faith. Sri Chinmoy speaks of 'Thy will be done' as the highest prayer that the Saviour Christ has taught us. One has to grow into depending on God for every little thought and action, at every second and to feel that one needs God alone.

The Sunlit Path: The Path of the Heart

At this point I should say that I experience the spiritual life as a journey full of joy, happiness, fun and so forth. Divine and childlike fun, but still fun.

I do not wish to convey the idea that the spiritual life is austere, but, yes, it is difficult. *'Life's perfection road is very long'*, says Sri Chinmoy, in one of his many aphorisms, *'but the journey is richly rewarding.'*

Most of us as Sri Chinmoy's students would say that we have had many laughs, chats, fun, played games, told jokes and so forth in the presence of the Master. Some of these are covered in *A Glimpse into the Personality of Sri Chinmoy.* (Chapter 5). Still, all spiritual life admits of discipline and struggle. It is its very nature. One has to be a divine hero, a warrior, fighting against the forces of temptation, greed, ignorance, etc., all the time transforming the negative impressions of the past.

Now the Sunlit Path is the Path of the Hero. It emphasises positivity, dynamism, going forward, courage, intensity and so forth. Naturally it becomes of paramount importance that one leads a positive lifestyle which includes diet, self-control and exercise, as well as many other virtues. While Sri Chinmoy was in the physical, on our Path there was always intensity. *'Why waste time'?* He used to say. He spoke of the Here and Now, The Eternal Now, what the Christian mystics referred to as the Sacrament of the Present Moment.

In our Guruji's teachings, there is no past or future; one is always in the Eternal Now. So we try always to live in the present, to be always doing something divine. This may include running, swimming, and other forms of exercise or serving others in a very dynamic and enthusiastic way. He used to say:

> "There is no such thing as future, my children. My sweet children, there is only Here and Now. Try to grow in the immediacy of today. Try to live in my Vision-Boat and my Reality-Shore. Like me, try to remain always in the Eternal Now. Grow in me, glow in Me, flow in Me. The Eternal Now is the only reality. He who aspires discovers the Reality of the Eternal Now."
> *The Oneness Of The Eastern Heart And The Western Mind, Part two, P. 464, (2004),* Agni Press.

Speed is also of the essence and there is no such thing as rest, no Saturday or Sunday. Rest is simply change of work. One needs to be always in the moment. Again, Sri Chinmoy says that it is when we take rest that the forces of temptation, destruction and ignorance come to visit us, to attack us. Yet this loving human being could be even gentler than a lamb. He knew our capacities, and taught us only in so far as we were able to receive. Of the Sunlit Path, he said:

"The Sunlit Path emphasises the positive way of approaching Truth. We have limited Light, now let us increase it. Let us progress from more light to abundant light to infinite light." *The Illumination Of Life Clouds, Pt. One, (1974)*, Agni Press.

Again, readiness, eagerness and willingness are very important. Consider the quotation below:

"At each moment you can be the happiest person both in heaven and on earth. The Supreme's universal consciousness and transcendental conscious can be your constant, illumining and fulfilling friends, if you want to have them as your own. You have to do only one thing: give what you have and what you are. What you have is willingness, and what you are is eagerness. Willingness and eagerness: Your willingness to become entirely His, constantly His and your eagerness to be utilised by Him at every moment in His own way. If you give these, then you do not have to give anything else. Then you will become His unparalleled, eternally unparalleled instrument." *Ten Divine Secrets, P. 18, (1987)*, Agni Press.

Of the Sunlit Path, Sri Chinmoy taught us that Truth is to be lived and defended. That there is no compromise between the aspiring life, and the unaspiring life. One needs to choose like a divine hero, and without compromise, offer up everything to the Supreme. For him ours is a heroic Path. Here we have to fight against doubt, obstruction and other negative or hostile forces in the way. But if our love of God is there, then everything becomes easy and safe. This he feels is the easiest, swiftest and most fulfilling Path for the sincere, totally dedicated and brave souls who are ready to walk, march and fly along the path of eternity.

Acceptance.

Sri Chinmoy spoke of his Path as the Path of acceptance. He taught us that the hoary days of living in the Himalayan caves are not valid any more. That the 21st Century is very dynamic and so we need to accept the world. The potter first accepts the clay, moulds it, and eventually it becomes a beautiful vase. In the same way, spirituality is not an escape from the world, but an acceptance of life in totality, with a view for the transformation and the manifestation of the divine Truth here on earth. This has to be done at God's choice hour and in God's own way. Consider this:

"Our philosophy is the acceptance of life, for the transformation of life and also for the manifestation of God's light here on earth, at God's choice Hour, in God's own way." *A Day In The Life Of A Sri Chinmoy Disciple, P. 61, (April 2008),* Agni Press.

This acceptance is further emphasised in the following two quotes:

" .. In our Path of acceptance, we have to know that the earth is far from perfection. Unless we accept the earth consciousness, how are we going to perfect it? If someone has some pain, I have to massage him. Then only will his pain go. Similarly, earth is defective at a particular place. I have to touch it with my aspiration and concern. Then only can I transform it"

"Our Yoga is the yoga of acceptance. If you do not accept anything, how are you going to transform it? The potter deals with a lump of clay. If he does not deal with the clay and soil his hands, how can he change the face and transform it?" *The Life Of Sri Chinmoy, P. 11; 47, (1984),* Agni Press.

For Sri Chinmoy, the spiritual and the life of real Yoga, was synonymous. In this yoga the world has to be accepted as it is. Waiting for the improvement of the world, for a better world in which to offer light, he likened to waiting for eternity. In its wisdom, spirituality does not wait. It knows that the world is evolving and progressing. So too, we are all progressing as human beings:

"Some are progressing slowly, while others are progressing fast, and still others are progressing very very fast. He who has an intense inner cry will naturally run the fastest. We have to accept the world and change the face of the world, transform the world of desire into the world of aspiration and transform the world of aspiration into the world of illumination and perfection. Acceptance-song we must always sing. We have to sing the acceptance song inside the body, inside the vital, inside the mind, inside the heart. Anything that is given to us by God, the Author of all good, must be utilised properly, Him to serve in His own way." *The Oneness Of The Eastern Heart And The Western Mind, Vol Two, P. 454, (2004)* Agni Press.

Consequently, practically all Sri Chinmoy's students, including myself, live in the world and work for the world as well as our own salvation. This way, as our inner Light increase, so too we enhance the Light in others and the evolution of mankind.

Sri Chinmoy asks us to give due importance to the physical. The body is the instrument of the Spirit and as such has to carry out its work. If it is sick and ailing, then we cannot pray and meditate well. Besides, it houses the Soul, which is the direct representative of the Supreme:

"On our Path we give due importance to the physical life. Inside the physical is the Soul which is the direct representative of God. The body is the temple, and inside the temple is the Soul, the shrine. But the shrine and the temple must be kept in proper order. We feel that our own inner life of aspiration and our inner life of dedication must go side by side. Like the flower and its fragrance, they cannot be separated. They have to be taken as two complementary realities. *Sri Chinmoy Answers, Part 10, P. 5, (April 1999)* Agni Press.

The Heart.

Sri Chinmoy teaches that his is the Path of the Heart. The Path of the Heart is the safest Path. The Heart is expansive, spontaneous and all-loving. This Heart – spiritual Heart – is like a child: sweet, innocent, pure and all-embracing. It thinks in terms of feeling, experiencing and oneness. The Heart speaks of 'we' and 'ours' whereas the Mind, which is quite different, speaks of 'me' or 'I'. It is the nature of the mind, according to Sri Chinmoy, to analyse, to separate, to feel supremacy, whereas the Heart is all harmony and universal oneness. The Heart, he feels, is the best medium for true communication. Here is a cute definition of the Heart:

"The Heart means oneness. The Heart is something that is always expanding itself by receiving light. The Mind, on the other hand, is not receiving light like the heart. Most of the time, it is unconsciously limiting and binding itself. The Heart is like a flower. The flower is not only beautiful but also fragrant. As soon as we see a beautiful flower, we get tremendous joy. Then when we smell its fragrance, our joy increases even more. When we enter into the heart, first we feel its beauty, and then we smell its fragrance. This is what the Heart is like." *Sri Chinmoy Answers, Part 19, P31,* Agni Press.

He continues: "The Heart is oneness, universal oneness."

"If we meditate on the Heart, and in the heart, then we will bring to the fore our inner light, which constantly tries to be of service to aspiring mankind … real spirituality, real meditation, real Yoga, is all inside the Heart. In the Heart is our ceaseless cry, our ever-mounting flame that reaches up to the

Supremes' transcendental smile, and then comes down to offer its inner wealth to aspiring humanity and to the world at large. "The *Oneness Of The Eastern Heart And The Western Mind, Part One, P. 72, 73, (2003),* Agni Press.

"The Heart only wants to establish intimacy and oneness with others; it gets satisfaction not in division, but in unification" *Sri Chinmoy Answers, P. 10, (1999),* Agni Press.

Sri Chinmoy has given a location of the Heart so as to help seekers along the way:

"The true spiritual Heart, about four finger-breadths in width, is located approximately twelve finger breadths directly above the navel, and six finger-breadths directly below the centre of the throat. It is here that one feels what you have called the 'quickening' of the Soul." *Yoga And The Spiritual Life, P 122, (1977),* Agni Press. For our Guru, Time was of the essence. The following prose expresses this:

> "Every day we must feel that it is our last day to realise God. Then sincerity will dawn. Otherwise, for Eternity we will walk along our Path and we will never reach our destination." *Transcendence Of The Past, (1977),* Agni Press

"Every day must come to you as a new hope, a new promise, a new aspiration, a new energy, a new thrill and a new delight. Tomorrow will dawn and you have already seen thousands of days? If you think that tomorrow will be another day like those which you have already seen, then you will make no progress. You have to feel that tomorrow will be something absolutely new

Sri Chinmoy in contemplation

that you are going to create in your life." *Inner Progress and Satisfaction-Life, (1977),* Agni Press

"From my Captain my eagerness has learned to see every second as the birth of a new day, and in it the complete life of a new year to please Him in His own Way." *Captain, My Captain, (1994),* Agni Press.

'Don't waste time. Do as much as you can. Before it leaves the body, each soul feels sorry that it has wasted time." *Reincarnation and Evolution. (1977).* And finally:

> "While you are meditating, you have to aspire all the time; otherwise you will fall. You cannot remain motionless at one point. In the spiritual life, movement has to be constant. Either you move forward or you move backward. If you try to remain motionless, the ignorance of the world will pull you right back to your starting point." *Meditation At The United Nations, Vol. One No 11, P 29,* (1973) Agni Press.

Aspiration and Manifestation

Aspiration and Manifestation are perhaps the 'building blocks' of Sri Chinmoy's philosophy. Yes, we need an unshakable faith in Something Higher, and we most certainly need Love, Devotion and Surrender. But Aspiration and Manifestation drive us forward and are very much part and parcel of the journey. So what are they? According to my understanding of Sri Chinmoy's teachings, Aspiration is an inner yearning, longing, or earnestness for the Divine Truth. It is an inner cry for more Light; abundant Light … Its nature is to rise higher, highest into the ever- transcending beyond.

The child cries for its parents, and they come running. So too, if we cry for God and our intensity is strong enough, then God comes running towards us. Sri Chinmoy teaches that the journey begins and ends with Aspiration. So Aspiration is crucial to progress in the spiritual life. So first we aspire, that is to say, first we pray and meditate, and whatever God gives us, we then manifest or express it to the spiritually hungry world; thus serving the God within ourselves and others. Let us allow Sri Chinmoy to tell us in his own words in the quotes below:

> "Aspiration is a cry within our heart. As a child cries, so also in the Heart you will feel a cry. A child is within you, shedding tears. He is weeping because he wants to transcend himself. This mounting cry, this climbing cry inside our Heart we call Aspiration.

When we aspire with our hearts tears, we see that God is coming down to us from above. The Heart is crying and yearning like a mountain flame burning upwards. The flame of the Heart wants to go beyond the mind, so it is always rising, and God is constantly descending with His grace, like a river flowing downwards. Ours is the flame that always burns upwards; God's grace, like a stream, is coming down from the Source." *Grace, P. 24,* (2003), Aum Publications.

"Aspiration is the burning glowing flame within. It is a birthless and endless flame, that mounts high, higher, highest and purifies the things that have to be purified in our unlit, obscure, impure nature" *The Oneness Of The Eastern Heart And The Western Mind, Part 1, P. 5, (2003),* Agni Press.

For Sri Chinmoy, aspiration has no beginning and no end. It is a constant mounting flame. The greater the flame, the greater our march towards our goal. Our only goal is progress, our inner assurance of a deeper manifestation. Aspiration is of extreme significance in Sri Chinmoy's teachings. Here are some more examples:

"In the spiritual life, there is nothing and there can be nothing more important than Aspiration. Aspiration is our inner cry for the highest Absolute. Aspiration is the eternal road. Aspiration is the eternal guide. Aspiration is the transcendental goal ..."

" ... Aspiration is the acceptance of life and the transcendence of death. Aspiration is the transformation and transcendence of the death force. Through our aspiration, we try to establish a free access to the immortal life, so that here on earth, we can establish the Kingdom of Heaven..." *(Ibid. p.579).*

" .. Aspiration is the very breath of God which we utilise for our own sake. Again, aspiration is the death of the ignorance of millennia. When ignorance comes to an end in a seeker, God claims that particular seeker as His chosen instrument, and God manifests Himself on earth through that seeker ...."

"... Aspiration expedites man's journey towards the transcendental goal, and accelerates God's manifestation here on Earth ..." *(Ibid. p. 60.)*

"Aspiration is our inner cry to reach the highest pinnacle of truth, Light and Bliss. Aspiration is the only key that can unlock God's door." *(Ibid. p. 171).*

To conclude, here is an ideal of Aspiration in Surrender:

"A man of aspiration says to God, 'O Lord, take me. What I have is for you, what I am for you. What I have is an inner cry, and what I am is unlimited ignorance. O Lord, do take what I have, and what I am." *(Ibid. p. 63).*

It is important to mention at this point, that the desire life is very different from the life of aspiration. Desire is related to the things of the material world. While it also has tremendous power, it is earthbound. Its nature is to grab and possess. There is no end to desire and it ultimately leads to dissatisfaction. Here we have the Master speaking to us thus:

> "Aspiration consciously follows the road of Light, whereas desire consciously or unconsciously follows the road of darkness. Darkness means satisfaction in limitation. Our desire wants to grab and possess, but before it possesses, it is possessed … desire embodies power which very often ends in frustration; and this frustration gives birth to destruction and annihilation."

"Desire is the product of our thought-waves; aspiration is the product of our Soul's will." *The Oneness of The Eastern Heart And The Western Mind, Part 2, P 257 - 258 (2004),* Agni Press.

Sri Chinmoy's teachings are extensive, and so the reader is urged to delve much more into the Master's 1600 or so books. I started off by expressing a desire to give you my reader, only a glimpse into Sri Chinmoy's philosophy. I hope that I have inspired you a little, as other books did for me in my spiritual infancy of some 30 years ago. Sri Chinmoy was very unusual in that he utilised so many different ways to serve, what still are today, predominantly western seekers, and as such he created new avenues for us all the time. However, by utilising his disciples, he has also reached millions worldwide.

While he taught us the Eastern approach of *Bhajans* to some extent, our Path includes lots of Manifestation – our soulful, selfless and dedicated service to humanity, to God; to our Guru's mission. So such things like soul-stirring musical concerts to invoke inner peace, physical activities, athletics, world harmony runs, singing, exercise, humour and many other endeavours, are quite common to us. (See Chapter fourteen, Part 2)

There was also dramatisation of the lives of Buddha, Christ and others, humanitarian projects and self-transcendence feats such as swimming the English Channel, or the 3100 mile race, which a few disciples ran. Sri Chinmoy would always find a joyful way to challenge our mental concepts of our own capacity. Needless to say, these activities served only to bring our spirituality to the fore and to expedite our progress.

As a final point, there are quite a few virtues which are paramount to Sri Chinmoy's philosophy. Here are some key ones: obedience, dedication, discipline, dynamism, enthusiasm, soulfulness … I will finally add purity and gratitude, both of which Sri Chinmoy has referred to as life-breaths of the Supreme. They will, with additional merits, again be highlighted in succeeding chapters.

This concludes Chapter Eleven. We have looked at God the Supreme, and the goal of life as well as touching on Love, Devotion and Surrender; the Path of the Heart. We have looked at the indefatigable cry necessary to reach God and its manifestation or expression of love to the Supreme here on earth and there in heaven. Let us finally end with a quote on Sri Chinmoy's philosophy to the world:

Sri Chinmoy on His Philosophy.

"Each individual must try to feel that he is, she is, a unique dream of God. If I feel that I am a unique dream of God, then I shall try my very best to do well in everything, because at that time I am linked with God, with my Inner Pilot. He is dreaming in and through me, and I am His dream. Whether I am five years old, or an octogenarian or I am ... always we have to think that we are children in the heart of God, in the heart of God's Creation, and God is watching us. In His Heart-Garden, He is watching us, whether we are playing with His flowers. So many countless flowers, countless flowers.

These are all human beings, so my philosophy is that, if in one sentence I can tell you about my way of life. Love God, serve God. Love God the Creator, love God the Creation equally. Love God the Creator, love God the Creation as well, equally, then God is bound to be pleased with us. We cannot separate them. The Creator and the Creation must go together. Love God the Creator, serve God the Creation, then we shall be able to fulfil God in His own way." *A Meeting With Sri Chinmoy, Part1, Video.* (2008) Mridunga.

- Manatita January 21st, 2012

CHAPTER TWELVE

More Wisdom-Pearls at the Feet of the Master

"The highest knowledge is the knowledge of one's conscious, constant, and at the same time, ever-transcending oneness with the Inner Pilot."

- *Sri Chinmoy.*
A God-lover's Earth-Heaven-Life, Part 3, (1974) Agni Press.

On the Humble Way

In this chapter, I will speak about certain ways and teachings of the Master. They may seem separate, but they will all help to enhance the readers understanding of Sri Chinmoy's methods.

In his relationship with, and dialogue with dignitaries, luminaries and numerous others, Sri Chinmoy was like humility incarnate. Speaking in his native Indian accent, sometimes softly, but always articulating well and with an excellent command of English, he would always say to the reverential: "I have come to be blessed by you." "Please bless me, Father." This approach was also used for women counterparts and other religious devout." To dignitaries he tried to bring forward their best qualities, to re-enforce how they were serving mankind and thus lift them in this way.

"I am grateful that you have given me the opportunity to be of service," He sometimes said. "I am so proud of what you are doing to serve others.", and sentences of a similar nature. This humble approach with bowed head or folded hands and attentive eyes and smile, was to remain with him all his life. He was all about seeing and bringing out the best in others, and taught his disciples to do the same.

On Religion

One could see Sri Chinmoy adjusting to western ways by the way he sat and how he answered questions. His strength and conviction in teaching, his voice tone, and his views on religion were quite touching. For more than forty-three years he continued to say that his was not a religion, but a Path. 'Ours is love of God', he stated, as well as giving many more wise and visionary answers. This is put quite eloquently below:

> "I belong to no sect and to no religion. At the same time, my teachings embody the quintessence of all religions. I admire and appreciate all religions, but I do not belong to any particular religion. I was born as a Hindu; therefore I know all the ins and outs of the Hindu religion. But I do not practice Hinduism. I do not follow any specific religion. My religion is to love God and to become a humble instrument of God. The Hindu religion is like a house, Christianity is another house; Judaism is another house. We can each live in a different house, and then come to one school to study. Spirituality, Yoga, is what we eventually must study." *Flame Waves, Part 11, P. 25. (1978),* Agni Press.

There is a school of thought called *Vedanta* in the East, which, even with all its purity, some still interpret as saying that the universe is unreal. For our Master, there is no such thing as an unreal world. The Universe is God's body, he maintains, and *Maya* (attachment or illusion, believing the phenomenal world to be the real existence) is part and parcel of the plan. This is illustrated below:

> "As my body is real, even so is my God's Body, the World. Nothing comes out of an empty void. God has projected the universe out of His Existence-Consciousness- Bliss. He has created the World. He has become the World. He wills, and He becomes. He smilingly unveils without what He is silently within" *Songs Of The Soul, Page 54, (*1971) Agni Press.

On Love for Children

As is common to men and women of God, he shared a great love for children and loved seeing their performances, showering them with lots of gifts from time to time. He took a great interest in their performances, and attended many. In keeping with his relentless activities and little sleep, our Guru had a great gift for recovery, and he could indeed come out of what would appear to be a short doze, to one of extreme alertness. The Master spoke of children thus:

"Children are nothing but fresh and beautiful flowers ready to be placed on the altar of God the Truth, God the Light and God the Delight." *Soulful Questions And Fruitful Answers,* (1976, Agni Press.

On Devotional Singing and Its Qualities

Sri Chinmoy spoke of God alone, and was always faithful to what he called his 'Inner Pilot' or 'The Supreme'. He consequently taught a lot of devotional songs towards this great Cause. He often sang impromptu, and would ask the singers to do notations or sometimes to learn just by practising in his presence. He also whistled songs. Over the years, he spoke of singing qualities which he wanted us to make our own when singing his songs. They included: consciousness, oneness, sweetness, soulfulness, confidence and perfection.

As time went on he would add more: correctly, prayerfully; cheerfulness and freshness; gratitude, as well as devotion and self-offering. I think it's necessary to pause here so as to give my reader a flavour of what Sri Chinmoy meant by consciousness and soulfulness:

"The difference between consciousness and soulfulness is: consciousness spreads; it is vastness, all-embracing, but soulfulness goes deep. When you are soulful, your whole being is going inward, inward, inward. Just think of consciousness as the ocean and soulfulness as the deepness inside. Consciousness is like a very huge, vast tree. Soulfulness is inside every branch, every leaf. Soulfulness is very deep, and in its depth you will find the whole tree. Consciousness and soulfulness go together like the beauty and fragrance of a flower." *A Day In The Life Of A Sri Chinmoy Disciple, P. 30, (2008),* Agni Press.

Sometimes Sri Chinmoy would suggest that we 'pull' on the song and at other times, depending on the nature and flavour of the song, he would say: 'soulfully and cheerfully, in a singing and dancing mood', and other such suggestions to the delight of the disciples. He had a wonderful way of bringing out the best in others. He knew exactly how to teach his disciples and who was capable of doing what on any given day. Needless to say, this brought out the best in his students, and made them excellent in their chosen area of work or manifestation. This ability to teach and give instructions according to capacity and receptivity, he would practise ceaselessly and effortlessly, until his Mahasamadhi on October 11th, 2007.

On Imagery

In his dress style, as well as his art-work, Sri Chinmoy made use of lots of beautiful colours, blue being his favourite colour. That sense of colour was also carried to his imagery in writing where he quite frequently used the analogy of a flower-garden with different flowers, or of different trees. Speaking of imagery, the Master made use of this quite powerfully, sometimes drawing vivid references to animals such as tigers, lions, elephants, camels, deer, and so forth. This was quite useful in so many ways to clarify or demonstrate an essential Truth to his many friends and devotees, as well as disciples.

On Truth

While Sri Chinmoy was all for telling the truth, he did not advocate a cruel or unkind Truth. The following aphorisms illustrate this:

"A painful truth is worse than a lie. Truth that hurts, truth that destroys Is no truth.
Truth that illumines, truth that reveals, Truth that perfects, truth that transforms
The animal in us, and satisfies the human in us,
And fulfils the divine in us, Is the only Truth."

Dedication-drops, Poem 37, (1976), Agni Press.

"Use your wisdom!
At times, on the earthly level, By telling only the truth,
We run into endless problems"

Seventy-seven Thousand Service-Trees, Part 50, 49,284.

"The truth that deliberately hurts- Mercilessly hurts-
Is worse than falsehood."

Seventy-seven Thousand Service-Trees, Part 50, 49,299.

Still, it is essential to tell the Truth:

Truth and I are Friends
A sleeping flower is my heart.
Believe it or not,
I tell only the truth.

Truth and I are indispensable friends.
A sleeping leaf is my mind.
Believe it or not,
I tell only the truth.

Truth and I are inseparable friends.
A sleeping lion is my vital.
Believe it or not,
I tell only the truth.

Truth and I are eternal friends. A sleeping dog is my body.
Believe it or not, I tell only the truth.
Truth and I are eternal friends.

The Golden Boat, part 7, (1974), Agni Press.

On Miracle-mongering

Sri Chinmoy was not fond of what he called miracle-mongering. While they may have been necessary at the very start of one's aspiring life, he feels that at a certain point one has to abandon them as they are unnecessary and can hinder one's progress on the journey. For him:

"Only two miracles are worth seeing:
The miracle of loving
And
The miracle of forgiving"

According to him, the greatest miracle is to remain one extra second more in a divine consciousness; the most illumining and fulfilling miracle is:

"To see and feel the infinite beauty
Of my Beloved Supreme Inside
the tinier than the tiniest
Gratitude-heart of mine."

Although miracles serve the purpose of fascinating the mind, Sri Chinmoy says that they create tremendous confusion and detract from the spiritual reality. In a way, a yearning and seeking or crying hear t is the greatest miracle:

"I do not need miracles, please,

I do not even want to see miracles, please.

I need and expect only

A crying heart and a smiling life"

Ten Thousand Flower-Flames, Parts. 54, 61, 66, (1983), Agni Press.

On The Importance of Time

In *A Glimpse Into The Personality of Sri Chinmoy* in Chapter 5, I have mentioned the importance of time. This is so significant in Sri Chinmoy's teaching. Life is like a flowing river, moving all the time and waiting for no one. So one has to avail oneself of all opportunities. The prose and aphorisms below illustrate this:

"So we have to feel at every moment that time is passing by. The river of time waits for nobody. We have to throw ourselves into that river and swim across it, to arrive at the destination." *The Master And The Circus Clown, P. 30, (2005),* Agni Press.

"The most important thing is to give importance to time. Never think, oh, there is plenty of time. No. You have to feel there is no time, no time. If you can truly feel that the river of time waits for nobody, then that very feeling will keep you more alert, more eager, more dynamic and more energetic to do the right thing" *The Master And The Circus Clown, P. 31, (2005),* Agni Press.

"We must not ignore life's fleeting moments,

For each moment is a golden opportunity

To arrive at God's door."

Seventy-Seven Thousand Service-Trees, Part 50, No. 49,222, (2009), Agni Press.

In the early eighties, we had very intense devotional practices with Sri Chinmoy. This included rising early in the morning, going to bed late at night and rising again early next day. We sometimes had very long meditations with our Guru, but he ensured that we had breaks in between. Some of us slept and waked at special functions, and then there was either the scolding or the occasional joke about such practice.

One never knew which would come. Yet, on reflection, how I missed that intensity, and so many of my spiritual brothers and sisters say the same. For the Master, beyond the mind, barriers do not exist. The mind likes to go from one to two, but according to him, why not go from one to ten if there is Grace?

"But why go from one to two if there is something called Grace? Why not go from one to ten? Fortunately, I have succeeded many times with this approach." *Aspiration-Body, Illumination-Soul, Part 1, (1993), Agni Press.*

Again, as mentioned previously, with Sri Chinmoy, everything is in the sacrament of the present moment, and so urgency and intensity he constantly made use of, as he pushed us in different ways to manifest God, the Supreme. Time, to our Guru, is of utmost importance. If we misuse time, the wrong forces will enter into us. So it is always paramount to act in the present moment:

"Life has only one Supreme motto:

Here and Now"

Seventy-Seven Thousand Service-Trees, Part 22, No. 21,362, (2001) Agni Press.

On Running The Fastest

According to Sri Chinmoy, the road is always ahead of us; life is always movement, even with the things we share, and movement itself is manifestation. We should not stop, but continue and continue. We have to increase our peace into abundant peace, boundless peace. He feels that in the act of transcending our achievements, we transcend our limitations as well.

"Life is always movement, movement. If I have something, then it must go from me to you and from you it has to go to somebody else"

The Master And The Circus Clown, P57, (2005), Agni Press.

One should always feel that one is moving, marching; running. Always new, like a newborn: "Always feel that you have just been born, then you will make the fastest progress. A little baby is always making progress – he is crawling, he is standing, he is walking, he is marching, he is running. Never think of the past – your past failures, past defeats or past imperfections. Feel that the past does not exist. Feel that only today, here and now, exists in your life. Do not carry anything with you from the past – whether it is good or bad

– if you can sincerely feel that you have just been born, that you are only a few hours old, and that you are on the lap of the Supreme, that He is responsible for you, you can make the fastest progress" *Sri Chinmoy Answers, Part 14, Page 30,* (2001), Agni Press.

"In your life, always try to see which way you can run the fastest. Always run the fastest, run the fastest, run the fastest! If you see that there is an obstacle on one way, then immediately give up that way and go another way, another way." *Sri Chinmoy Answers, Part 26,* (2000), Agni Press.

On Self-giving

I have already touched on self-giving. A lot is covered in Sri Chinmoy's beautiful book called *The Wings of Joy.* Still, for those who may not have read this book, The Master says that the game of creation is interdependence. The greatest joy is to give another a part of our hard-earned achievement. Whatever we share after we have gained increases immeasurably and our hearts become full of joy.

We were encouraged to and gladly helped with serving in disciple enterprises such as restaurants, health food shops and so forth. Here one cleaned or swept or did the washing up or helped in other ways. Guru used to say that human nature does not grow and cannot grow without selfless service, and to this day it is extremely important to our Path.

"When you feel that what you gain from your aspiration is for humanity at large, then your heart becomes wide and receptive" *Cry Within: Yours Is The Goal,* (1974), Agni Press.

One should also be happy; doing everything happily, one would have no regrets. A seeker's gratitude would increase for his Master through self-giving. According to Sri Chinmoy, self-giving increases our receptivity. We should only give and give and give. By so doing, we would find ourselves flooded with the Master's joy, blessings, light, love and gratitude. This message we can find in many of his books. Below is a most lofty poem by Sri Chinmoy on giving from the heart:

"Wherever you go, go with inspiration and aspiration.
Whatever you do, do with love and concern.
Whomever you see, see with purity's beauty
And responsibility's glory."

Arise, Awake: Thoughts Of A Yogi (1972), Agni Press.

On working with others, the Master suggests that we become as humble as possible. That we try to exercise our wisdom rather than our justice. He asks us to try to be at the other person's feet, not on his head. This will avoid any increase in disharmonious situations. One needs to be humbler than a blade of grass, to feel that one is not indispensable to a project. Success or progress depends on God. One simply needs to do one's best, and the feeling of supremacy should be discarded.

Guruji exhorts us to always show appreciation to others. Should we wish to inspire others, to raise them up, one way is to bend, to lower our own height so that the other person can climb on top of us, metaphorically speaking. According to our Guru, without humility, it is impossible to have harmony. Let us share his thoughts on humility:

"You have to absolutely make yourself feel that you are as humble as a speck of dust or a grain of sand. You have to become the embodiment of purest humility, and feel that you are nothing but a speck of dust, and that you are placing this worthless thing at the Feet of the Supreme" *My Heart Melody,* (1994), Agni Press.

I will conclude with a supreme definition of selfless service by Sri Chinmoy:

"Anything that you do to become soulfully one, devotedly one, unreservedly one, unconditionally one with the Will of the Supreme, is selfless service. If you can do the highest form of meditation on the psychic plane, mental plane and vital plane, then you are doing the best form of selfless service …" *Service Heroes, (1978),Cited in Disciples Companion, P. 203,* Agni Press.

On The Necessity of Manifestation

Perhaps unique to Sri Chinmoy was the assertion that the three stages of God- realisation, God-revelation and God-manifestation, were all necessary in the divine scheme of things, in order for perfect perfection to dawn on Earth. Here to describe the same, the Master used the analogy of the mango tree. Let us say, perhaps, that life is a rather long journey, and that we are actually climbing a very tall tree. Naturally this is a difficult task and may take some time. The realised Soul is the one who is surer of foot, swifter, stronger and with a greater intensity to get there, so he gets there first (God-realisation).

At the top of this tall tree there are many mangoes. The Realised Soul foregoes the bliss at the top of the tree to come down again and share with his other brothers and sisters who are not so strong. First he tells them that there are mangoes on the tree, and then he reveals it to them (God-revelation). Next he takes out a knife from his pocket, cuts a slice or slices, and shares it with them. (God-manifestation). Sri Chinmoy teaches that until the individual manifests God, his role is not complete and perfection does not take place.

"If I do not climb up God the tree, then I remain unrealised. If I do not climb down with the fruits, then God remains unmanifested. Perfection dawns only when I am realised and God is manifested" *My Rose Petals, Part 1V*, (1974), Agni Press.

"God-revelation is the promise made by God-realised souls on the strength of their unconditional concern for suffering humanity.

God-manifestation is the unconditional promise of God-realised souls to love mankind unconditionally and to manifest the reality of Divinity here on earth." *The Oneness Of The Eastern Heart And The Western Mind, Part 1*, PP 130, 171, (2003), Agni Press.

Sri Chinmoy puts all this very nicely in the next quote:

"We have to offer our realisation in the form of Revelation to mankind. Revelation is also not enough. We have to enter into the domain of manifestation. If we do not manifest what we have here on earth, if Mother earth does not receive the fruits of our realisation, and if she does not have it for good, we can never be truly fulfilled.

Mother Earth has to be fed with the fruits of our realisation. Here on Earth, the manifestation of realisation has to take place, and when manifestation takes place, perfection is bound to dawn. Perfect perfection is nothing other than the absolute manifestation of God's transcendental will here on Earth." *My Rose Petals, Page 18, (European talks,* (1970), Aum Publications, 1971.

On Gratitude

There are a few more areas of Sri Chinmoy's teachings, which, while they may have been expounded by others, are nevertheless of paramount importance and noticed quite easily in his many manifestations. First there is Gratitude: gratitude to the Supreme and gratitude to the Supreme in humanity. To him, gratitude as a most soulful prayer or a most soulful meditation embodies everything. Gratitude is the life breath of the Supreme. This is reflected in a great many of his songs. Here are two examples: *'My own gratitude heart is all that matters'; 'I want to see every day, a gratitude-sun in my heart,'* or the aphorisms:

"The most beautiful thing on earth is our heart's gratitude to the Supreme, to the divinity in humanity, to God. This is the best and most valuable thing on earth. This is the beauty unparalleled, and it will remain so throughout Eternity." *A Galaxy of Beautiful Stars,* (1974), Agni Press.

Gratitude is not a mere word; it is not a mere concept. It is the living breath of your real existence on earth. Sri Chinmoy's Talk on Gratitude, Jan 16th, 1994.

"Gratitude is not a mere word.
Gratitude is not an idea. Gratitude is not even an ideal. Gratitude is our hearts
God-satisfaction promise
To God Himself"
Twenty-Seven Thousand Aspiration-Plants, Part 193, (1993), Agni Press.

Throughout his life Sri Chinmoy expressed his gratitude to us and to his numerous guests through gifts, inner spiritual experiences and in many, many wonderful ways. He also taught us to do the same for others. He was never known to forget an action, or to overlook showing his gratitude, and indeed frequently showered us with gifts, particularly children and on special events such as birthdays. One had the feeling that he always remembered when one did something nice, even if it was a year or so later.

On Physical Fitness

Then there is the question of exercise, already mentioned in Chapters 5 and 7. For our Guru running is very important. It is a continuous motion, showing us that there is a goal and offering us the message of self-transcendence. If we neglect the physical, Sri Chinmoy feels that the body and the mind would become weak. Consequently, it would not have the strength to focus on good things and would be attracted by the undivine. So many disciples run, walk, swim, climb mountains and do other sporting activities such as our World Harmony Run (see Chapter 14, Part 2) on a regular basis. I myself have participated in and assisted with many Sri Chinmoy marathons, swims and world harmony runs in many countries.

World Harmony Run closing ceremony, Vienna.

On Newness and Speed

Change and urgency are also important to our Master. For him one always has to go forward with new ideas. To do things in a new and creative

In training

way. To enhance or develop oneself, newness and freshness were always important to him. "Why always follow the old system?" He used to say. Again, things should be done with speed, quickly and without procrastination. One should not say, 'I will try'. One should simply do. There should be no "how", but "I am doing it", not, "I will/want to." Where there was a sense of collective oneness, and identification with a Higher Source, then security and confidence would come. Never to give up under any circumstances he suggested should be the motto of one's life.

This sense of urgency, immensity and intensity; this offering of the inner man, one should utilise not only to help oneself, but to elevate the consciousness of each individual on earth. Again, others who are yet to come to earth in future incarnations, would also be helped, Sri Chinmoy feels. He encouraged us to:

"Look forward,
Run faster than the fastest.
Past years are like
Used and torn garments."

Seventy-Seven Thousand Service- Trees, Part 13, poem 12, 777. (1999), Agni Press.

On Being Like A Child

Being like a child is very important. God is a divine child who is always playing with us, and according to our Guru, we ourselves have to become like children in order to play with Him. We could do this best by being in the heart, by relying upon God with a child's heart. The Heart is the best medium of communication. This he feels quickens our progress, and increases our peace, light, love and bliss. Those who want to make the fastest progress should follow the path of motherly love. To do so, faith is extremely necessary.

Sri Chinmoy laughed a lot with us. 'Laugh at the world, laugh at your stupidity, laugh at your responsibility and laugh at everything', he used to say. In this way, we can relieve the burden that is on our shoulders. Innocent fun takes away all our tensions, he feels. If something takes away all our tensions, worries and anxieties, then it is as good as meditation. So in his presence we often had innocent, sweet, pure and simple fun.

On Evil

For our Guru, evil is only a form of lesser Light. This simply means less perfection, less illumination, but is also part and parcel of the higher plan. God is the only Doer.

"Evil is a force that has less light or insufficient light. Anything that has insufficient light we call a harmful or destructive force. Anything that has light in a very insignificant measure and, at the same time, does not add to our divinity, we can call evil. But from the real spiritual point of view, there is no such thing as evil; it is only that something is less perfect, less illumined and less fulfilling." *The Disciples Companion, Vol 2,* (2006), Agni Press.

On The Significance of Soulful Singing

Sri Chinmoy wrote volumes of songs, and singing is essential in the Sri Chinmoy Centres for invoking the qualities of a great many of our Guru's songs: peace, light, bliss and other virtues. Music in its highest form is meditation. Not the everyday music of the world, but music which is devotional, which expresses a sublime yearning for something Higher, the Heart's yearning to be free. We sang a lot around Sri Chinmoy, a practice which is still of paramount importance to Sri Chinmoy Centres all around the world. Such singing most certainly helps me in my collective meditations, and in my own environment. Of his songs Sri Chinmoy says:

"Each time you sing a song prayerfully, soulfully, self-givingly, plus correctly, I clearly see inside my heart-garden, a new flower with tremendous beauty and unbelievable fragrance in your heart of aspiration"

"My spiritual songs are part and parcel of my aspiration and my God-realisation ... I wish to say, with all my sincerity, that my songs are playing a most significant role in my life history, and also in your own life history, whether you are singing or you are listening" *(Talk on Singing at Aspiration-Ground, 30 August, 1993.)*

On Fate

On Fate Sri Chinmoy teaches that it is not the last word. That fate can be nullified; it can be changed by an unchanging will; that the soul in man is greater than his fate and that all can be done if the God-touch is there. This is reflected in some of his songs from words which were written by his Master Sri Aurobindo. On nullifying fate he says:

"There is a world which is infinitely higher than the planets. From there we can easily create, and we can also delete anything in our fate. If we delete what is there, then we can add something new. Your fate can also be adjusted by the Grace of the Supreme. If a seeker is very highly developed and gets considerable Grace, either from God or from a great Spiritual Master, then the planets cannot influence that seeker. Even if one is an ordinary seeker, if the Master intervenes, then the planets cannot do anything.... God's Grace can change anybody's fate. This Grace is almighty; it changes the occult possibilities and transcends the laws of astrology, which are God's cosmic laws"

"If you have total faith in your aspiration and in God's Grace, then you need not worry about your future." *Grace, Page 34-34, (2003),* Aum Publications.

Still personal effort is necessary, he feels, as it expedites the descent of God's Grace to earth.

On not Being Bound by Plans

According to Sri Chinmoy, God is not bound by any law, and changes his plans from time to time. Perhaps the following authoritative prose will help us to understand why destiny is not the last word:

> "From the highest spiritual point of view, everything is predestined and again, everything is not predestined because God Himself is not bound by any law. He is eternally free ..."

"On the one hand while creating the universe, God has made certain laws so that there will be some system, some order. But in His case, every rule admits of exception. If he blindly sticks to His own principles, then He is like us. We need certain disciplines, certain principles so that we will arrive at a certain point, a certain goal. But in God's case, He is the starting point and He Himself is also the goal. So He does not have to adopt the human method that has to do such and such in order to get the results. If in His Vision He sees something, then the Vision will be transformed into reality. But on the way, if He wants to change the Vision itself in order to arrive at another reality, then He can do so.

So God is not bound by anything. Since He is not bound by anything, we cannot say that everything is predestined. It is predestined for the fatalist, for one who believes constantly in fate. But there is a superior force, an infinitely superior force, and that force is called the Grace of the infinite Supreme. So God's infinite Grace can easily nullify, expedite and illumine fate and do anything that it wants to do in order to better the consciousness of humanity ...*" Dipti Nivas,* (Cited in *Disciple's Companion, Vol 2, P.202, (2006). (1976),* Agni Press.

On Creation and Evolution

Here I will give the seeker a glimpse of Chinmoy's views on creation and evolution. This is important to the seeker in so far as it sheds light on reincarnation and the immortality of the Soul. It is also useful as it gives a sense of involution and evolution for those who may not yet have read some of the works of the Master pertaining to these areas. This is perhaps best understood from the standpoint of what the Master calls Consciousness, the spark of life which connects each of us with the Universal Life. The thread that puts us in tune with the universe:

"Consciousness is the spark that lets us enter into the Light. It is our consciousness which connects us with God. It is the link between God and man, between Heaven and earth." *Beyond Within, P. 3, (1985)*, Agni Press.

On Creation our Guruji says:

" … Creation enters into inconscience and then gradually comes back to its Source, and remains its Source. When it enters into inconscience, into the lowest chasm of reality, we call this involution. And when from the lowest chasm creation again climbs up high, higher, highest, we call this evolution. The silence God has another name: Spirit. And the sound God has another name: matter. Progress requires involution of Spirit, and evolution of matter." *The Oneness Of The Eastern Heart And The Western Mind, Part 1, (2003)*, Agni Press.

The next quotations explain this even further and are testaments to evolution and re- incarnation. Sri Chinmoy has also written a lot more on these subjects in his book *Death And Re-incarnation*.

"We know that we started our journey from the mineral life, and then entered into the plant life. Then we entered into the animal kingdom. From there we have come into the human world. But here is not the end. We have to grow into divine beings. Unless and until we have become divinised and transformed, God will not be satisfied with us. He can manifest in us and through us only when we are totally transformed and fully illumined. So when we think of our evolution – inner evolution and outer evolution – we get abundant joy. We lose nothing, nothing in the so-called death.

Jalalu'd d-din Rumi most beautifully and soulfully tells us about evolution:

A stone I died and rose again a plant.
A plant I died and rose an animal;
I died an animal and was born a man.
Why should I fear? What have I lost by death?" *(Ibid. p. 119)*.

We finish with a quote from Sri Chinmoy in a very simple and lucid style:

"The day we left the animal kingdom, we started our spiritual journey. After passing through the plant kingdom, we entered into the animal kingdom and our evolution went faster. Then from the animal kingdom we entered into the human kingdom, and our evolution became conscious. Now from the human kingdom, we are consciously, soulfully, devotedly, divinely and unconditionally, trying to enter into the divine kingdom." *(Ibid. p. 140).*

I have crammed into this chapter quite a few gems of Sri Chinmoy's teachings, and this should give you, my reader, an even better sense of his life's philosophy. I would say, though, that while one may feel running through it, a thread of urgency, speed, intensity and a constant forward movement, somehow Sri Chinmoy's Path came with, and still retains its sweetness, as brought to us by our beloved Teacher. Consequently, even in the most ardent struggle, for my part and for most disciples that I have spoken to, the joy remains.

– Manatita 9th March, 2012.

CHAPTER THIRTEEN

A Glimpse Into Sri Chinmoy's Teachings on Purity.

"I have to know that each thought that I think is a prayer. I have to know that each action that I take is a meditation" - *Sri Chinmoy*
My Rose Petals, Part IV, Section 1, The Aspiring Life, Paragraph 3, (1974), Agni Press.

I was born and brought up in the Christian faith, and as such I have read about and become familiar with some of the chaste people of my Faith. Still, I learnt quite quickly to be prudent in talking about the celibate life. Somehow, it makes some people feel insecure, inadequate. Others feel and are usually able to give numerous examples as to why God wants us to procreate. The life of continence or abstinence is an unwelcome challenge for some of my friends, Christians and non-Christians alike. It is with this in mind that I am endeavouring to show that this is not something new. Speaking on this topic, The Christ says:

"For there are some eunuchs, which were so born from their mother's womb: and there are some eunuchs, which were made eunuchs of men: and there be eunuchs, which have made themselves eunuchs for the kingdom of heaven's sake." *The Holy Bible: King James Version. Matthew Chpt. 19, V. 12*

St Paul, whilst giving counsel to the Corinthians, first recognises that every man has his gift from God. He then goes on to encourage us to be like him, or if not, to take up the legal status of marriage:

"For I say therefore to the unmarried and widows, it is good for them if they abide even as I. But if they cannot contain, let them marry: for it is better to marry than to burn." *The Holy Bible: King James Version. 1 Corinthians, Chpt. 7, V. 8 – 9.*

The great God-Man of the 19th Century, Sri Ramakrishna, speaks with authority:

"When the mind becomes pure and is freed from worldly attachments and longings, one comes to have true yearning, and then alone will your prayers reach the Lord. No message can be sent if the telegraph wire be broken or if there be any other interruption" *Readings On Swami Brahmananda's Spiritual Teachings. P. 94, (1993)* Ventura Publisher, Athens, Greece.

His beloved disciple Swami Brahmananda says it even more directly:

"We need tremendous energy for leading a higher life, and this energy of ours, which is really one, cannot be wasted through sexual channels, if we really want to progress and attain something … No, whoever desires to lead the higher life must pay the price fully. There can be no bartering in this." *(Ibid. p.72).*

In my relationship with my friends, I used to point them to the richness of my Faith: of the many monasteries and institutions in Christianity dedicated to the search for God. These include the Desert Fathers, the Order of Carmelites and Cistercians, the Order of Jesuits and Franciscans; the Trappist Monks and others.

Finally, I reminded them of the pictures of the Saints which adorned the walls of many houses of devotees of Christ, and of the pious lives they led: Padre Pio of Petronella, St. Francis of Assisi, St. Augustine of Hippo, regarded by some as the Father of Christian spirituality. Also St Theresa of Avila and her contemporary St John of the Cross, Therese Neumann, the German Catholic Stigmatist, St Theresa of Lisieux, Julian of Norwich, and the more modern contemplatives such as Meister Eckhart, Thomas Merton, Father Bede Griffiths, who led an Ashram in India, and of course our dearest Mother Theresa. My friends would at first be surprised at my knowledge, then, being reluctant to discuss further, would walk away.

Before I give you, my reader, a glimpse into Sri Chinmoy's teachings in the light of what I have discussed so far, let me just say that in our Christian spirituality, most of us see Monasticism as Chastity, Poverty and Obedience. In Yoga philosophy, however, it is interpreted as purity of thought, purity of words and purity of actions, ultimately even in the dream state. So purity, it seems, would cover all three vows and chastity is simply part of the process. It is useful to bear this in mind as I would sometimes speak mostly of lower desires, with purity being brought in as necessary to support the argument. Sri Chinmoy speaks of Chastity thus:

"Chastity means inner purity, inner beauty. If we enter into our heart-garden, there we see the heart as a flower and we see that this flower has tremendous fragrance. If we see a flower, first we appreciate the beauty of the flower. Then if we see that flower has fragrance, we appreciate that flower more. Here, inner beauty is chastity. If we are pure, then we feel that our inner beauty expands and our inner fragrance increases.

In the spiritual life, we try to please God as much as possible. If there is a way to please God more, then we try to adopt that particular way. The necessity of chastity is not only my philosophy, other spiritual Masters, as well as the Saviour Christ have given so much importance to chastity, because they know that if we have chastity, then we can make very fast progress. Chastity, inner beauty and inner purity expand our divine reality" *Sri Chinmoy Answers, Pt. 19, P. 35, (1999),* Agni Press.

Sri Chinmoy's view of the subject, while essentially supportive; while maintaining the necessity of an inevitable transformation of the lower Vital (see Chapter six), in my humble view and experience, nevertheless takes a slow and steady approach:

"A seeker cannot achieve inner purification all at once. It is a gradual process. Inner purification begins with our conscious meditation; then it has to be achieved during our waking hours; then it has to be achieved during our sleep. After all these it can be done in the dream state. We have to start at the beginning and work in sequence. That is to say, during meditation, we have to purify ourselves constantly. It is useless to attempt meditation without purification, and it is useless to expect purification without meditation." *Purity: Divinity's Little Sister, PP. 4-7, (1974),* Agni Press.

Or this second more direct quote:

"I am not telling you that you have to give up your lower vital life, your sex life, all at once. No, if you do that, it will only destroy your health, destroy your whole inner existence. You have to give it up slowly and steadily. But the day has to come; the divine day has to dawn when you will give it up completely. If you think that sex life and God-realisation go together, then I cannot help you ... gradually you have to transcend your sex life because

God-realisation and sex-indulgence can never go together." *A Hundred Years From Now, P 28 – 29, (1974),* Agni Press.

In Sri Chinmoy's philosophy, celibacy has to be achieved only through the proper method. First inner purity has to be established through a life of spiritual practices. He feels that the seeker has to gradually abandon his lower vital life, through many years of practice in order to be fully celibate. Sufficient purity has to be established first. The following quote alludes to this:

"If your vital is not ready, if it is not pure enough, it will revolt under this harsh discipline and destroy your aspiration, or your body will resist and break down. If you suppress your vital needs without having sufficient purity, then after two or three years, or even after a few months, they will come forward again most vehemently." *Purity: Divinity's Little Sister, PP. 25 – 33, (1974),* Agni Press.

According to Sri Chinmoy, before running fast in the spiritual life, it is of paramount importance to have the necessary capacity and preparation, without which the seeker will become exhausted and will have to give up the race. Nevertheless, to enter into the life of the lower vital for the beginner seeker, every day means entering into the very jaws of a devouring tiger. The seeker is encouraged to try to minimise. How could the seeker do this? The next quote is also an example of a slow and steady approach:

"How can we acquire celibacy in the proper way? We have to gain control gradually and naturally. Vital indulgence is just like drinking or smoking cigarettes. If we have a drink or smoke a cigarette seven times a day, then we must diminish gradually; we must make it five, four, three, two, one, and then none. Why? Because these things carry misery: they are like slow poison, weakening our inner life and delaying our realisation. If we gradually diminish our desire to drink or smoke, we will be successful and will not damage our health." *(Ibid).*

Again, as a part of the same process of purity, Sri Chinmoy lays emphasis on cleanliness, physical purity, a wholesome life-style to include vegetarianism and freedom from alcohol, smoking and drugs, unless given by one's doctor for medicinal purposes. He feels that all these things do damage to the subtle spiritual nerves. Our Guru also encourages the necessity of a proper shower or bath at least once a day. Water signifies consciousness, purest consciousness, according to him, and bathing helps the seeker to go immediately to the purest consciousness within. Still, it is important to realise that the inner purity is vital to all things external. Consider the following quotes:

"True physical purity lies inside the heart. You have to establish an inner shrine within your heart. This shrine is the constant remembrance of the Supreme Pilot inside you. When you constantly and spontaneously think of the Supreme Pilot seated inside you, in the inmost recesses of your heart, you will realise that this is the highest purity. If purity is lacking in the physical, complete success, the full manifestation of God, cannot be accomplished ... Purity is not something weak or negative; it is something soulful and dynamic. It is something that is fed constantly by the infinite Energy and indomitable, adamantine Will of the Supreme." *The Oneness of the Eastern Heart And The Western Mind, Vol 2, P 76, (2004),* Agni Press.

"You actually kill your inner being when you live an impure life. But when you live a pure life, you expedite the journey of your Soul. Your Soul and your outer life get their greatest opportunity when purity is totally established in your life." *(Ibid).*

"The real purity comes from the inner aspiration from the Soul, not from food. If we have some spiritual purity, then the physical purity that we get from not eating meat will be most effective. If we do not have purity, no matter how carefully we abstain from eating meat or fish, purity will not come to us." *Purity: Divinity's Little Sister, PP. 4 – 7. (1974),* Agni Press.

Now like all Spiritual Masters, Sri Chinmoy answered questions at different times from different seekers in different ways. It is consequently important for the reader- seeker to understand that I can only explain his writings and talks as I perceive them. So when I say that he appeared to meet people at different levels, then kindly bear with me. The disciple, for instance, as I understand it, is meant to be at a level in tune with the Master's wishes. So while the slow and steady approach would naturally be of paramount importance to the disciple, he/she is still meant to be pursuing a path of discipline and transformation. Certainly, I have been practising celibacy for some time, and my understanding over many years is that my brother/sister disciples are walking along this same road.

Sri Chinmoy always encouraged wakefulness, discrimination. Sure enough 'boys' and 'girls'[1] meet together and work together for the manifestation of Sri Chinmoy's mission. We also socialise. Still, we use the traditional way of yoga philosophy for sitting at all our functions. That is to say, 'boys' would sit on the right side of the Master, with girls on the left. It is important to recognise though, that in Sri Chinmoy's teachings, we are all equal before God. So while discipline is certainly needed to run our international Centres, Sri Chinmoy did not encourage hierarchy or separation in a negative way.

Still, as protecting one's inner purity is of the utmost importance, wisdom dictates vigilance, watchfulness and other noble virtues along the way. Sri Chinmoy saw purity as the life-breath of the Supreme. However, I need to emphasise that, from my own experience, our Path is not austere; there is a very loving and a pure and joyful relationship based on oneness, a sense of inner connection with the Master and the disciples, and with the Master's mission.

God is first and foremost in the disciple's life, and as such we try to avoid lower vital forces (the emotional life) which may affect us, create uncertainty and a solid wall ahead. So we grow together through dispassion, vigilance, through our aspiring consciousness; through the Soul's Light; our oneness with Sri Chinmoy ...

From my experience on purity and in listening to and reading the Master's writings, there seems to be a gradual approach to purity, which is ever progressive, and can be considered in stages. Sri Chinmoy explains thus:

"Those who have just awakened should try to purify their lives slowly. Those who are a little advanced must be very careful and give all attention to their spiritual life. Those who are really advanced find that lower vital necessity does not enter into them. For them the life of pleasure is replaced by the life of real joy." *(Ibid).*

Here is another:

"For the beginner, I say, 'slow and steady wins the race.' As he advances, as he makes progress in the spiritual life, automatically, the necessity for lower vital activity diminishes. Until then, one should do his best to lead a pure, sincere life, according to his own standard. Once the aspirant reaches the point where he can say, 'I want infinite Light, infinite Joy, infinite Bliss, infinite Peace; I want to go far, farther, farthest', then he must pay all attention to purifying his vital life.' Sri Chinmoy continues:

"If his aim is God-realisation, the Infinite, the Eternal, the Immortal, then he has to aspire wholeheartedly: physically, vitally, mentally, psychically, with all his existence, with all that he has and with all that he is. At that point he has to become totally celibate not only physically but also mentally. He has to feel that the sex life binds him to the lowest level of earth-consciousness, whereas what he wants is the highest God-consciousness.

God is inside earth and inside man. But man will be able to function divinely, only after he has surrendered all his ties to earth and man, and realised his oneness with God." *(Ibid. pp. 25-33).*

So we see here that struggle is necessary, and that one has to fight like a divine hero. Sri Chinmoy teaches that as a divine warrior, we have to use our dynamic power to fight against fear, doubt, worry, ego, insecurity, jealousy and other negative movements:

"At every moment you have to feel that there is a battle going on between your aspiration and the pull of the material world. So you have to be more careful, more vigilant, and more spiritual." *Sri Chinmoy Speaks, Part 8, P. 4 – 6.* (1976), Agni Press.

"Without purity he cannot retain any of the spiritual gifts he receives. Everything will disappear and everything will disappoint the seeker if he is wanting in purity. But if he is flooded with purity, the divine qualities will all eventually enter into him. They will sing in him, dance in him and make him the happiest person on earth. And by making him happy, these divine qualities will find their own true fulfilment." *The Oneness of the Eastern Heart and the Western Mind, Vol 2, P. 76,* (2004), Agni Press.

Sri Chinmoy's Path accepts married couples and encourages those who are one- pointed in their search for life's meaning. Here, according to Sri Chinmoy, marriage shows that two can easily become one, that a sense of separativity can be transformed into unity and oneness. It is God and the individual who should make the decision. There is no hard and fast rule.

Here mutual faith, mutual love, mutual sacrifice and mutual self-giving are the ingredients for a successful spiritual marriage. These can be supported by purity in thought and action, patience, both in the inner life and the outer life, and always to live in the loving heart rather than in the doubting mind. *(Ten Divine Secrets. (1987)* Agni Press).

So we see that the transcendence of the lower vital – the sex life – is of utmost significance. Whether one is single or married, the same principle ultimately applies. All energy eventually has to be God-centred., and a life of abstinence is essential for Self-realisation. We see also that Sri Chinmoy speaks to different seekers at different times but that the message conveyed, according to my understanding, is that a slow and steady process is the key, depending on one's capacity, relationship with God and inner awakening.

Finally, I would leave my reader with a more vivid and practical quote from Sri Chinmoy:

> "If you drink five cups of tea daily, then try to drink only four for a few weeks. Then make it three and after a few weeks make it two, then gradually one. If you try to stop drinking tea overnight, it will tell on your health. The best thing is to go slowly and steadily in the process of spiritual growth. One knows how often he indulges in vital life. Gradually, he should try to curb his vital movements, because his ultimate goal is to drink Nectar, immortal bliss. Slowly and steadily, he has to march towards the goal."
> *Aspiration-Glow And Dedication-Flow 1, P. 6 – 7, (1977),* Agni Press.

-Manatita 3rd February, 2012.

CHAPTER FOURTEEN

A Glimpse Into the Legacy of Sri Chinmoy (Part 1)

"By providing the opportunities for individuals and communities to express their hopes for peace, you strengthen the social, cultural and spiritual fabric that connects the entire world family. Young people, as well as older individuals, will discover new ways to bring forward the best in each of us, ways we have yet to imagine. Encouraged to make their unique contributions, all members of the world family, will help to move our dreams closer to reality. All these efforts, can renew our shared commitments so necessary in this sometimes troubled world" *–Dr Davidson Hepburn, President, UNESCO General Conference. http://www.youtube.com/watch* (last viewed 22nd May, 2012.)

In the above passage, Dr Hepburn is talking about the 25th Anniversary of the Sri Chinmoy Oneness-Home Peace Run/World Harmony Run, founded by Sri Chinmoy in 1987. He is remarkable in his vision, and indeed speaks eloquently, expressing the ideals for so many of Sri Chinmoy's other manifestations; so many endeavours. The Sri Chinmoy Oneness-Home Peace Run is just one of these.

I once read somewhere, that God-men and women, wherever they are, use their indomitable Soul's will, to project loving and compassionate blessings, soulfully reaching and serving mankind. This apparently happens whether they are in Himalayan caves or in the material world. Sri Chinmoy lived in the world, and his way was to accept it and to work for its transformation and manifestation, while in the world. In his forty-three years of service in the West, he certainly visited hundreds of places and a great many countries in the pursuit of world harmony; in the pursuit of peace.

All this has been expressed outwardly and is continuing to manifest in the hearts and minds of those who love him dearly, and in others whom his friends, admirers and well-wishers are still continuing to inspire. They include

Kings, other luminaries, politicians, dignitaries, and world bodies such as the United Nations, sportsmen and women and numerous others.

Some of them are now running their own programmes and are reaching out to others in God's own way. Whether it is Tegla La Roupe, or Sudhahota Carl Lewis, or politicians like former President Gorbachev or Nelson Mandela, they all say that Sri Chinmoy was a remarkable man, and felt inspired by him in one way or another. Certainly I travelled with Sri Chinmoy on a lot of these goodwill and peace-building trips, and saw at first-hand how he worked. He was always giving; offering ceaselessly day and night. Extending love to his students and to the world at large.

Sri Chinmoy with Nelson Mandela and President Gorbachev

Today the disciples are utilising this vast energy flow carried over as an act of love from Sri Chinmoy, and utilising this spiritual stream to serve others. They do so in a variety of different ways, from initiatives either started by Sri Chinmoy –who was incredibly versatile and prolific – or through other ideas again inspired by him. I begin with the Sri Chinmoy Oneness-Home Peace Run/World Harmony Run, which has reached millions of people in over 140 countries. It has done so by spreading the simple message, through a flaming torch, of love, harmony and universal oneness. Of the Run Dr Hepburn has said that:

- It encourages both young and older individuals to discover creative new ways to bring forward the best in each of us, ways we have yet to imagine.

- By visiting world heritage sites, it encourages people to experience and value the heritage of others.

- It fosters a culture of peace and a growing feeling of universal-oneness through inter-faith initiatives.
- The Torch-bearer Award programme inspires others to emulate and build upon their own important contribution.

- It is imperative that we work together to build a true oneness world. Among recent initiatives to strive towards this goal, the World Harmony Run is one of the most remarkable and far-reaching.

The Sri Chinmoy Oneness-home Peace Run/ World Harmony Run

This amazing event was founded by Sri Chinmoy in 1987. It is a global relay that seeks to promote international friendship and understanding. As a symbol of harmony, runners carry a flaming torch, passing it from hand to hand travelling through many countries around the globe. To a large extent, the Sri Chinmoy Oneness-Home Peace Run appeals to individuals, because it does not seek to raise money or highlight any political or religious cause, but simply strives to create goodwill among peoples of all nations. Towards this cause Sri Chinmoy's students, friends and admirers, have visited schools, parliaments,

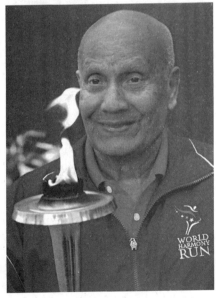

With World Harmony Run/ Sri Chinmoy Oneness-Home Peace Torch

churches, towns and cities, and have even sent the Torch on a journey into space.

Original Sri Chinmoy Oneness-Home Peace Run Director Shambhu Neil Vineburg

Sri Chinmoy always felt sport to be a powerful vehicle for promoting global harmony, international friendship and understanding. Towards that end, he ceaselessly and tirelessly worked, bringing together a great many men and women from all walks of life. This included Mother Theresa, a great advocate for peace and a saintly Mother to the suffering and dying in many countries through her Sisters of Charity mission. Other notable inclusions were Mohammed Ali, Reverend Desmond Tutu and many world leaders who supported this cause.

What was Sri Chinmoy's message for and vision of the Sri Chinmoy Oneness-HomePeace Run? This is his response to questions put by his students in 1987:

"There are many ways to become happy, but I feel that the easiest and most effective way is to run outwardly, so that we can remember our life's eternal journey. Life itself is a journey, when we run, we feel that we are running towards our goal and again we feel while we are running that we are achieving something. I give so much importance to physical fitness because inside the body is the Soul, which is the direct representative of God"

And again he uses an analogy that expresses the universality of the message of the run most effectively:

> "Everything goes from the one to the many. A seed becomes a plant; then it becomes a tree, and finally the tree produces countless fruits. So here also one thought goes to another individual and from him to a third person. From one, two, three, four, from one to many. The Creator was one, but He wanted to become many. How did He become many? By creating the universe and becoming countless, infinite human beings.

So when one person comes and offers the peace torch to another, we feel that God the Creator, who was one, is becoming God the Creation, who is many. It is from the one that the message goes to the many. Again, when the message is fulfilled, we see and hear the song of oneness. So it is a complete and perfect circle of oneness, oneness-home." *Taken from interview with Sri Chinmoy, Flushing Meadow Park, 1987.*

The Sri Chinmoy Oneness-Home Peace Run has been, in recent times, temporarily called the World Harmony Run. Today this run has grown stronger and stronger, spreading across the globe on the internet, on T.V and radio, through communities and across seas in a most powerful and remarkable way. Organised by an international network of volunteers, the WHR has its Headquarters in New York, USA, but there are many branches worldwide. Its members put on small events yearly and a larger more regular biennial run, supported by many around the globe. The American leg of the run generally involves a grand ceremony outside of the Dag Hammarskjöld Plaza in New York City in April of that year.

Present Sri Chinmoy Oneness-Home Peace Run Director, Salil Wilson

Sri Chinmoy Oneness-home Peace Run, 1999 in Togo, West Africa.
Back row right: Vishvarupani, Austria. Front: Denny, Canada. Adhirini, Switzerland, a
Togolese runner, myself and Ganapati. Teachers and pupils at the back.

My experience of the Sri Chinmoy Oneness-Home Peace Run, from the late eighties to the present, is that it has produced extremely touching and lasting memories of a variety of different kinds. Simply by being given the opportunity to touch the torch, and by making a wish for peace, many have been inspired and affected in numerous ways. The Sri Chinmoy Oneness-Home Peace Run serves as a powerful force to remove barriers along the way. This is reflected in the enthusiasm and cheerful smiles of teachers, the innocent joy and delight of children jumping and running for joy at the sight of us, or through our kids-to-kids- programme, developed to help them share with others in a creative and meaningful way across the globe.

Children with World Harmony Run, East Kuching, Malasia, 2009.

I recall running through Drogheda, Ireland, in the late eighties and then from Dublin to Belfast. In those days soldiers were still in camouflage on patrol at their check- points. I felt so moved to see them joining us, holding the torch, and running a few steps for world harmony! Of course one of the successes of the Sri Chinmoy Oneness-Home Peace Run is that everyone is involved. From grandparents to politicians, statesmen, luminaries and others of good will everywhere. There are no barriers in the sense that it is all about goodwill, sharing, and feeling happy in a most tangible way.

Abhijit, Canada, and Frank, France. With two Senegalese up front.

With that vision we generally achieve otherwise difficult things. This varies from getting police or armoured escorts to accompany us, supplied by various local authorities, to the setting up of peace dedications (Peace-Blossoms), by those who feel inspired so to do. I have personally witnessed many practicable benefits of the run, by people in authority, who had the good sense and the foresight to see its unending promise. Today, we are growing larger and larger, the vision is bigger, bolder, and we have lots of support and assistance from those who wish nothing but to assist with the fragrance and beauty of the Sri Chinmoy Oneness-Home Peace Run. So here we see the flowering of Sri Chinmoy's vision most powerfully taking place as expressed by him in the same talk:

"This Oneness-Home Peace Run is the very beginning of something infinitely, infinitely greater than we can ever imagine. This Peace Run is definitely not like other peace runs; it is not a whim or mental determination to bring about peace. The Peace Run is an unprecedented Vision that has come directly from the highest Absolute Supreme. It is not a man-made plan; it is God's transcendental Vision that has descended into the mind and the heart of the God-lover in me. I have transferred it to you, and now you are transferring it to the world at large.

From the Transcendental the message has come, and now you and I and other God- lovers are offering it to the universal. God the Transcendental has given us this blessingful Message to carry to His own creation; which is God the Universal." *(Ibid).*

Aklilu, Daulot and Devendra, WHR Ethiopia 2010.

I have run across fields, uphill and down valleys with the Peace Run, and all this is continuing today, four years after Sri Chinmoy's Mahasamadhi, and even as I write. I have travelled across the lakes of Togo, West Africa, run up Mt Kilimanjaro, Tanzania, and watched with joy the smiles and happy faces of so many children, local authorities, men and women, or as Sri Chinmoy calls them 'God-lovers', in many countries. I have even sat with the Elders in Abidjan, Cote "d' IVoire, and the Jumbe experts in Senegal, all in the name of harmony, togetherness and the spirit of universal oneness.

Start of the Great Ethiopia Run, 2008. Aklilu Gebrewold and WHR Team are up front.

Dipavajan Renner, Aklilu Gebrewold and elite athletes on Mt Entoto, WHR Ethiopia, 2006.

The message continues, being bigger, brighter and better, and serving most powerfully, as a vehicle of the Supremes' plan to express God's vision here on Earth. Finally, let us end with Sri Chinmoy speaking of his 1987 vision, which 25years later, and after his passing, has become so much a reality, in more ways than one.

"This Peace Run will be the supreme awakening of true and genuine God-lovers on earth. There are many on earth who want to be God-lovers but, for various reasons, have not yet become God-lovers. But with this Peace

Run they are getting the supreme opportunity to grow into God-lovers. The main contribution of this Peace Run is to bring together all the God-lovers, that is to say, all the lovers of God's creation. And those who are inwardly getting the message to become God-lovers and to serve God's creation will be amply helped by this run."

WHR/Sri Chinmoy Oneness-Home Peace Run, 1999. Mombasa, Kenya.

"This Peace Run is not only unprecedented; it is also the very beginning of something that humanity and Mother Earth will forever and forever treasure. With this treasure earth and humanity will be able to claim the transcendental heights of God as its very own. As this Peace Run covers the length and breadth of the world, we shall see how Heaven and Earth can go together, carrying the same message of the Creator's infinite Joy, which is inside His Eternal Peace." *(Ibid)*.

The Sri Chinmoy Oneness-Home Peace Run/World Harmony Run, has held nu-merous opening ceremonies outside of the Dag Ham-marskjold Building in Man-hattan, New York. The Run continues, as mentioned above, with its significant work, even to this very day.

World Harmony Run, Gostling, Austria, 2012.

Sri Chinmoy's Musical Legacy

Sri Chinmoy gave many musical concerts around the world. Nearly 800 in fact and these took place at many prestigious establishments such as the Royal Albert Hall, Carnegie Hall and the Sydney Opera House. Right from the beginning music has been important to our Master. Indeed Sri Chinmoy speaks of being blessed by Mother Saraswati herself. (Saraswati is the goddess of music and the arts). Sri Chinmoy saw music as the universal language of the heart, dissolving barriers of race, language and culture.

"It is through music," he said, "that the universal feeling of oneness can be achieved in the twinkling of an eye." *Sri Chinmoy Speaks, Part 4, (1976),* Agni Press.

Sri Chinmoy playing the cello.

Sri Chinmoy was a prolific composer with thousands of songs to his credit in his native Bengali and in English. He played many instruments from all over the world including a variety of flutes, the Indian esraj, cello, harmonium, piano and pipe organ.

Sri Chinmoy playing the piano.

Our Guru felt that soulful music could draw us beyond the limitations of the mind into the calm beauty of our own inner being. It was for this purpose that he gave many Sri Chinmoy Peace Concerts around the globe. The Master composed while in a meditative consciousness, and his music is imbued with a profound meditative spirit. Even at its most powerful, it contains an underlying stillness that reflects its source.

I myself have attended many of Sri Chinmoy's Peace Concerts, whether it was in Prospect Park, New York, in churches, and during the time of the Centenary of the Parliament of World Religions in Chicago in 1993. There he gave a most stirring concert in honour of Swami Vivekananda, a seer from his native land. I also attended the very first concert at the Sports Halle in Cologne in 1984.

Royal Albert Hall Peace Concert, 1984. Sri Chinmoy is standing prayerfully on stage invoking peace.

In all these concerts, Sri Chinmoy began prayerfully. Standing in front of the audience with his hands folded in supplication to the Supreme, he would always invoke a most powerful and tangible blessing from on High

This strong sense of peace was conveyed to the audience, and over the years we have had a great many comments from people who came away from such concerts totally filled with joy, peace and love. Of music Sri Chinmoy says:

"Music is the inner or universal language of God. I do not know French or German or Italian. But if music is played, immediately the heart of the music enters into my heart, or my heart enters into the music. At that time, we do not need outer communication; the inner communion of the heart is enough. My heart is communing with the heart of the music and in our communion we become inseparably one. In the spiritual world, next to meditation is music, the breath of music. Meditation is silence, energising and fulfilling. Silence is the eloquent expression of the inexpressible" God the Supreme *Musician, (1976),* Agni Press.

"Soulful music immediately awakens and inspires our hearts because it embodies the Absolute Supreme. Soulful music is the Light that wants to express itself in a divine way. Even as darkness wants to manifest its authority

Peace Concert, Auckland, New Zealand, 1989.

on Earth, Light also wants to manifest its Reality and Divinity in a specific way. Light is the soul of everything. Light is the soul of music, Light is the soul of love and Light is the soul of all art. When Light divinely manifests itself in the form of music, it is the music of the Soul." *(Ibid).*

Sri Chinmoy teaches that music means Self-expansion and oneness. The Self expands through music. The Self that expands is not the individual self but the unlimited Self, and that music is the expansion of unlimited Reality. Again, by listening to Sri Chinmoy's music at his Peace Concerts, one could not but feel the experience of Sri Chinmoy's soulful words below:

"When we listen to soulful music, or when we ourselves play soulful music, immediately our inner existence climbs up high, higher, highest. It climbs up and enters into something beyond. This Beyond is constantly trying to help us, guide us, mould us and shape us into our true transcendental image, our true divinity. When we hear soulful music, or when we play a soulful piece of music, we feel a kind of inner thrill in our entire existence, from the soles of our feet to the crown of our head. A river is flowing through us, a river of consciousness, and this consciousness is all the time illumined." *(Ibid).*

Chinmoy playing his Beena at the Great Wall of China, 2005.

Just one year prior to Sri Chinmoy's Mahasamadhi, he asked one of his students, Boris Purushottama Grebenshikov, to give a concert at the Royal Albert Hall. This went very well and the Master was very pleased. He consequently asked Purushottama to do another concert at the same venue the following year. The concert happened, and I have described it in Chapter three entitled Spiritual *Experiences*. We all felt Sri Chinmoy's presence very strongly, as if he was alive and with us on that very special evening in 2008. At that concert, Purushottama played with some of the members of Songs of The Soul, who have continued to perform since that time.

Songs of The Soul Ensemble, Royal Albert Hall, London, 2008.

The Title '*Songs of the Soul*,' was chosen from the Master's writings post his Samadhi, in order to celebrate, as well as express the depth, eloquence and inner experience of his music. This continues to be done with a full gamut of melodies, moods, styles and ensembles, which varies from time to time, depending on the availability in the different countries in which they are performed. The singers and musicians evoke a soulful and meditative atmosphere in their performances. Many members of *Songs of the Soul* are in The Gandharva Loka Orchestra, excellently led by Panchajanya Burri, a disciple of Sri Chinmoy.

It is worth mentioning that *Songs of the Soul* has attracted quite a few virtuoso and celebrity artistes, some of whom have actually met and performed for the Master. They include Additwiya Roberta Flack - singer, songwriter of jazz, soul, rhythm and blues - on piano, Phillip Glass –music writer and composer - and Boris Purushottama Grebenshikov, the Russian legend, who performed on guitar at the first *Songs of the Soul Concert* at the Royal Albert Hall, May 30th, 2008.

The name Gandharva Loka was given to Panchajanya Burri, during a Christmas trip to Bulgaria, in January, 2007. He was then asked to put a group of musicians and singers together and to perform for Sri Chinmoy in a couple of days. This he did, and the Master liked the performance tremendously. Since then, The Gandharva Loka Orchestra, which expanded to include many other musical artists, has toured Europe successfully and also many other countries. They perform with Songs of The Soul, in memory of Sri Chinmoy whose music has been described as incredibly magical and absolutely divine. They have enchanted audiences far across the globe.

Today, just over four years after the Master's passing, Songs of The Soul, that most remarkable ensemble, continues to perform the Master's music for large audiences in many countries. They have enlarged the group – well over 100 members - added rich and varied voices, accomplished or professional singers, and have even teamed up with Rezwana Chowdhury Bannya – a famous and distinguished Bengali trained singer – as well as her Shurer Dhara[1] Bengali singers.

Together they have performed in the Master's country, Bangladesh - very dear to his heart - at the Harmony Hall of Bangabandhu International Convention Centre (BICC) on December 13, 2009. They have appeared on State and National T.V. side by side with the Rabindranath Tagore[2] singers, singing both Sri Chinmoy's and Tagore's songs. Songs of The Soul reflects a musical journey, which takes the depth, power and sheer vastness of Sri

Chinmoy's musical compositions, and weaves an experience dedicated to the voyage of the human soul.

Sri Chinmoy had set up a great many other musical groups, and now there are even newer ones inspired by him. They tour various countries in Europe and around the world, and visit places where we have our Beautiful Peace Blossoms such as Cabo De Roca, continental Europe's most westerly point. They have also played at the cloisters of the beautiful Jerónimos Monastery in Lisbon. The concerts are played to small as well as very large audiences, and in the true tradition of our teacher Sri Chinmoy, are always free.

One such musical group that stand out is the Sri Chinmoy Bhajan singers. They are an international group of women singers and musicians from North America, Europe, Australia and Japan, who perform Bhajans – songs of God-souls - composed by spiritual teacher Sri Chinmoy. Most of the songs are written in Bengali but they sometimes sing English songs, which our Guru also composed.

The singers seek to create an atmosphere rich in devotion and to invoke humanity's highest yearning for inner peace. Superbly led by Ms Ranjana Ghose, their instruments vary from hammer dulcimer, tambura and flute, to the sarod, violin, guitar, synthesizer and bells. They are practically all accomplished musicians with soul-stirring and heavenly voices.

This wonderful and loving group continues to manifest Sri Chinmoy's legacy in a divine and sublime way. They also play to audiences at the United Nations, the ideals of which the Master held in the highest esteem. Just two weeks ago, on the evening of Saturday April 14th, 2012, they played in the company of other Sri Chinmoy musicians at the New York Society for Ethical Culture, near Central Park, in Manhattan, to an enthralled audience. I must say that as a fellow-seeker there on that memorable evening, their music was truly soul-elevating and I felt a blazing light of peace and experienced a remarkable inner beauty flooding my being.

I have already said that there are many other musical groups. They vary from Temple-Song-Hearts – an all-female vocal and instrumental ensemble - who also sing nationally and internationally, to Mountain-Silence, another all-female group, who give virtuoso and yet soul-stirring performances around the world. Then there is the all-male group who sings Sri Chinmoy's songs in their pure form without accompaniments, and play in vast churches in Iceland, Japan, Switzerland and elsewhere. There is also Ananda, another accomplished vocal and instrumental boys group, who perform our Master's music at retreats, universities and other serene locations around the globe.

Sri Chinmoy composed over 22,000 songs, each expressing an aspect of the myriad beauty and profundity of God's universal Grace, and the seeker's aspirations for the profound truth of being. The majority of these songs have been heard at some time or another, sung and performed by various artists such as Kailash's group, who were trained and guided by the Master himself. They have sung literally thousands of Guruji's songs, and are known for their tremendous outpouring of our Master's work. They do so to express their gratitude, to glorify, celebrate, embrace God's love, and invoke and share this unique experience of outflowing joy, with all whom they meet.

Literary Outpourings

By now, you, my reader, will have become familiar with the eloquence and profundity of Sri Chinmoy's prose and poems. To me it is a God-given gift which Sri Chinmoy showed or demonstrated, and which can be traced all the way back to the Sri Aurobindo Ashram. There it was noticed by Nolini Kanta Gupta – the poet savant – and Sri Aurobindo himself, both of whom encouraged Sri Chinmoy with his writing.

Sri Chinmoy's Birthday, 2005.

The Master was most certainly a prolific writer, producing a staggering 1600 books and more. They are composed of plays, short stories, jokes, questions and answers, and a great many more. Some books are about lectures and university tours, conversations with renowned or eminent people such as Princess Diana, Pablo Casals, Leonard Bernstein and many others.

Sri Chinmoy wrote an extensive number of poems of which some were done in series. These include Ten Thousand Flower-Flames, a 100-volume effort of 10,000 poems, 27,000 Aspiration-Plants, a 270-volume work of 27,000 poems, and 77,000 Service-Trees, which remained unfinished at the time of the Master's Mahasamadhi – a God-man's conscious exit from this world. The Master wrote Transcendence- Perfection, a collection of 843 poems, in 24 hrs.

Sri Chinmoy says of his writings that when sincere seekers read it with soulfulness, with love and devotion in their hearts, the Master becomes aware and inwardly helps them. I have personally experienced this sweet inner feeling many times through reading our Master's poetry and prose.

Over the years, Guruji would read to us from time to time from his aphorisms, poems, joke books, playful subway experiences and many others. It was a joy and a great inner thrill to listen to the Master by just being at his feet. There we were, sitting cross-legged or on benches or chairs, imbibing the Master's joke stories and laughing happily and profusely.

While mostly contemplative, Guruji sometimes laughed as well. It was such a joy and blessingful treat to sit in Satsang with the Master. Some of the favourite books read from were *Songs of The Soul, My Lord's Secret Revealed, Everest-Aspiration* and *Ten-Divine Secrets.* Others like *The Wings of Joy, Meditation: Man-Perfection in God-satisfaction,* and *Beyond Within,* were great inspirations to us, and are still sold at Meditation classes and public functions in many world-wide locations.

Sri Chinmoy gave about 388 university lectures in diverse places such as Harvard, Yale, Princeton, Oxford, and Cambridge, McGill, Moscow State and Tokyo universities. Many of these countries have Deans and other scholars who still remember Sri Chinmoy with lots of love. Today Sri Chinmoy's books can still be bought in a great many countries and are distributed in shops, libraries and bookstores all over the world. They serve as beacons of light, hope and inspiration to perhaps over a million people,

Sport and Athletics

I have been fortunate enough to be handed some competitive medals by Sri Chinmoy. They were given for first place in the 70-metres dash, and 3rd in shot-put and pole vault. They were also given for the 100 metres, 200 metres, marathon and others. All this came about through the inauguration of the Sri Chinmoy annual Sports Day in 1970 in New York. Sri Chinmoy would generally begin the event with a March Past, after which there would be numerous sporting disciplines to include sprinting, jumping and even tug-of-war. Guruji shared more than a great love for sport, and indeed it was part and parcel of his philosophy.

As with literature, Sri Chinmoy practiced sports and athletics at the Ashram in India, where he was the 100- metre sprint champion for 17 years. He was also the decathlon champion for two years. While there, he excelled at shot-put, pole-vault and running, among other sports. All this certainly supported the philosophy of Sri Aurobindo's Integral Yoga, and Guruji was to utilise sport as a vehicle for progress; for self-transcendence, quite early after his arrival in the West.

Finishing a race, Jamaica, Queen's

Almost from the beginning he suggested that his disciples take up running. They started from two miles a day and were eventually doing ultra-marathons. These two mile races were run around a one mile loop and soon became the famous Runners Are Smilers now called Sri Chinmoy self-transcendence races. They were among the Master's favourite races, and are still being held by many Sri Chinmoy Centres around the world. Sri Chinmoy has talked about running and self-transcendence in Chapter 7, but I would leave you, my reader, with yet another teaching from Sri Chinmoy, on why we do sports:

> "I feel that the world needs dynamism. The outer world needs dynamism and the inner world needs peace. As seekers, we have to pray and meditate in order to have peace. Again, if we can be dynamic, then we will be able to accomplish much in our outer life. To be dynamic we need physical fitness at every moment, and running helps us considerably to keep physically fit. Also, running reminds us of our eternal journey in which we walk, march and run along Eternity's Road to our eternal Goal." *The Outer Running And The Inner Running, Section 1,* (1974), Agni Press.

It was towards this cause of outer physical fitness, inner transcendence, not only for disciples but for serving the community, that the Sri Chinmoy Marathon Team (SCMT) was formed in the fall of 1977.

The Sri Chinmoy Marathon Team organises races and other events such as triathlons and swimming competitions, in many countries around the world. While the Team puts on races of all distances from two miles to a marathon, it has become well known for its pioneering work in organising ultra-running events (races of longer than marathon distance). Many of the races organised by the Sri Chinmoy Marathon Team have now become established preferences in countries in which they are held. The 24-hour races held in New Zealand, Switzerland and Great Britain are now all established national events.

The Six-and Ten-Day races held in New York every year are extremely popular races in the USA ultra-running calendar. In Australia, the SCMT offers an unparalleled range of multi-discipline events, including the famous Triple-Tri, a triathlon performed three times over in the scenic outskirts of Canberra. However, the jewel in the Sri Chinmoy Marathon Team's crown is the 3100 mile Self-transcendence Race, the longest certified road race in the world, which is run each year in Jamaica, Queens, New York, between June and August. The competitors seek to complete 5649 laps of a .5488 mile course (883 metres) in a time span of 52 days.

The SCMT's love of hosting endurance events is a reflection of the core philosophy behind the team's activities. The races are organised on the principle of self-transcendence, where each runner competes against himself and his own previous capacities rather than against his fellow runners. Endurance races allow each competitor to go deep within and truly find the best within himself/herself. In order to persevere and finish, and even though there are trophies for the leading finishers, in truth every runner who completes such long distances is a winner.

The Sri Chinmoy Marathon Team has gained a reputation for the level of care and support they provide to the competitors, in their races, raising the bar for their excellence in ultra-events. Many SCMT members have performed remarkable feats in different disciplines over the years, showing that indeed anything is possible if one just has faith in oneself. Perhaps the most well-known Sri Chinmoy Marathon Team member is Ashrita Furman, who currently holds over 100 Guinness World Records in many disciplines, including the fastest five miles run on stilts (a record which had previously stood for over 100 years), and the fastest mile for crawling.

Sri Chinmoy has many disciples who do phenomenal and inspirational things. Until recently, Suprabha Beckjord, a woman from Washington DC, held the distinction of being the only person to finish the 3100 Mile Race for every year that it was run, a total of thirteen times until 2009. Karteek Clark from the UK has swum the English Channel ten times now; and the forty or so successful attempts by SCMT members at crossing the English Channel make it the team with the most English Channel crossings.

Every year in Munich, Germany, the Sri Chinmoy Marathon Team hosts the Impossibility-Challenger event in which specialists in unusual disciplines from all around the world, arrive to try and achieve records in their respective fields.

Sri Chinmoy, the Founder of the Marathon Team, was himself a frequent marathoner and ultra-marathoner in the seventies and eighties, and was setting records in the field of weightlifting right up to his Mahasamadhi on October 11th, 2007, at the age of 76 years.

Sri Chinmoy has sought to show how sports can be harmonised with the spiritual life. He teaches his students to use sport not as a way of defeating others, but as a means of progress, of transcending their own limitations. He also tried, by example, to inspire athletes young and old to do the same. Sri Chinmoy completed 22 marathons and 3 ultra-marathons. His fastest marathon time was his first marathon in Chico, California, in which he clocked a time of 3:55:56. Often he would go training as early as 4am in the morning.

Today the Sri Chinmoy 3100 mile race is the world's longest certified race. It takes place on a one mile loop around the suburbs of Jamaica, Queens, New York, and it's known for its organisational expertise, friendly runners, helpers and team. Sri Chinmoy encourages us to:

"Run and Become, Become And Run, Run to Succeed in the outer world, Become to proceed in the inner world" *The Outer Runner And The Inner Running, (1974),* Agni Press.

Again, perhaps to inspire us, and with his usual vision, Guruji, in his composition of our World Harmony Run song, tells us "You are the oneness and fullness of tomorrow's sun.'

Weightlifting and Other Athletic Endeavours

In 1985, a knee injury curtailed Sri Chinmoy's running career, and he turned his attention to weightlifting. This was a sport in which previously he had shown little interest, but right from the beginning of his weightlifting career, he was able to make unprecedented progress. Up until his Mahasamadhi, in October, 2007, at the age of 76, Sri Chinmoy continued to lift a unique variety of different weights.

At the age of 55, after only a little over a year's training, he lifted 7063¾-lb as a one- arm lift with his right hand. Not long after, Sri Chinmoy lifted 7040¼ -lb. with his left hand also. Bill Pearl, five times Mr Universe, has acted as Master of Ceremonies at many of Sri Chinmoy's weightlifting ceremonies.

Of his weightlifting, Sri Chinmoy has said that everything is 100% God's grace and God's compassion. It is not the physical, he has said, God wants to manifest in and through the physical, and the physical becomes an instrument for a Higher Light. The following quotes allude to this:

> "Only I want the manifestation of God's Will, to show that the spirit can be manifested in and through the body. Previously spirit and matter were separated. Matter was one thing and spirit was another. Spirit wouldn't touch matter; matter wouldn't touch spirit. Everything I have achieved is by virtue of my prayer, meditation and spiritual life. Now my Lord wants my prayer-life and meditation-life to work through my physical, earthly body in this way."

"Previously I used to say 99 per cent, but now I give 100 per cent credit to my Inner Pilot, who is my source of inspiration and aspiration." *Aspiration-Body, Illumination- Soul, Part 1, (1993),* Agni Press.

"I just use my prayer, my meditation and my surrender-life to God's Will. I pray and meditate and, at the same time, I surrender the results to God's Will. This is what I do. " *(Ibid).*

Today, Sri Chinmoy's weights and equipments are beginning to be exhibited around the world in mobile exhibitions supported by dignitaries and other known celebrity figures. There is a unique film called Challenging Impossibility, made about Guruji's weightlifting and incorporating his philosophy, particularly inspiring for senior citizens. This film is a 2011 documentary film, which chronicles the weightlifting odyssey of the Master. It shows him performing feats of strength by drawing from the source and power of meditation which comes as a result of his spiritual life; his devotion to the Supreme. The film also shows very eminent people paying tribute to the Master.

These lifts have been featured on newscasts worldwide, inspiring people to transcend their personal limitations and to abandon their concepts of the restrictions of physical age. Directed by Natabara Rollosson and Sanjay Rawal – both disciples of the Master - this film was an Official Selection of the 2011 Tribeca Film Festival and premiered April 22, 2011.

Sri Chinmoy honoured men and women of inspiration, people who had tried in different ways to be of service to others. This he did by lifting them overhead with specially built apparatuses for the occasion. The "Lifting up the World with a Oneness-Heart" programme, is a unique award that he offered, to recognise individuals from all walks of life who had inspired and uplifted humanity. The Master lifted the recipients overhead either with one arm or both arms, using a specially constructed platform in a symbolic gesture of oneness with their uplifting achievements. Of this he says:

> "I am trying with my capacity to encourage and inspire people in various walks of life that have inspired others in sports, literature, science or politics, or in their own personal lives. I lift them up to show my appreciation for their achievements."

Beginning June 1988, Sri Chinmoy honoured more than 8,300 individuals in this manner, including Heads of State, diplomats, spiritual and religious leaders of many faiths, distinguished achievers in the arts and in literature, Nobel laureates and world class athletes. He has said that:

"Only by our positive thinking,
By our bringing the positive qualities
Of others to the fore, Will this world be able
To make progress." – Sri Chinmoy.
Seventy-Seven Thousand Service-Trees Vol 15, No.14779, (1999), Agni Press.

Sri Chinmoy's disciples continue to swim, run, bicycle or take some active part in exercise, which plays a significant role in Guru's philosophy. We also do a 12 hr. walk every April in honour of the Master's coming to the West and a 47 mile race every August – started in 1978 - to celebrate his birthday. Judging by the many letters received, many athletes are inspired by our energy,

Manatita being lifted with a special apparatus

cheerfulness, endurance and dedication to the spirit of constant inner progress and self-transcendence.

So many times, when I reflect on these races, I can still see Sri Chinmoy standing there, coaching, smiling, encouraging, setting distances for us to run like two miles or even seven miles at the spur of the moment. Then again I hear the, "On your marks, set and go", followed by the cheers and clapping of the audience as we go surging into the distance. Again there are still the *Prasad* (food blessed by the Master), post races, the repeating of a soulful aphorism or two, read out after the event, and most importantly, the camaraderie by his disciples and friends, gathered together for these special events. The SCMT is highly respected around the world.

CHAPTER FIFTEEN

A Glimpse Into The Legacy of Sri Chinmoy (Part 2)

The Jharna-kala Foundation

Sri Chinmoy painted over 200,000 works of art since 19th November, 1974. Commencing 29th December, 1991, he drew nearly 16,000,000 soul-birds. Drawing of birds was one of his favourite subjects, at which he was very adept. To him they symbolised the freedom of the Soul. Here is one of his quotes about birds which re- enforce this perception:

"Birds have a very special significance; they embody freedom. We see a bird flying in the sky, and it reminds us of our own inner freedom. Inside each of us there is an inner existence we call the soul. The soul, like a bird, flies in the sky of Infinity. The birds we see flying in the sky remind us of our own soul-bird flying in the sky of Infinity. While looking at the

Sri Chinmoy's Soul-Birds

birds, feel that you yourself are a bird; you are your soul-bird flying   in the   sky   of infinite light, infinite peace and infinite bliss." *Sri Chinmoy Answers, Part 3, (1995),* Agni Press.

The soul-bird figures quantitatively throughout the creative works of Sri Chinmoy, and is distinctive of his style.

Sri Chinmoy with Soul-birds.

Sri Chinmoy refers to his art as "*Jharna Kala*," or 'fountain art' in Bengali – a spontaneous creative flow arising out of an inner stillness. They show the birds, some in flight, some in repose, each depicting the imagery and choreography of the human soul. They range in size from tiny miniatures, materialising on the page with a calm lyrical sweep of the pen, to large canvases rich with bright vibrant colours. The ink strokes are those of a master hand, deftly capturing soul-birds, each with its own personality, hovering alone, or in harmonious groups in an inner sky.

Ms. Ranjana Ghose, Curator of the Jharna Kala Art Foundation, has noted exquisitely that:

"Sri Chinmoy uses the language of art to express what comes from within, and one might observe that he utilises that language eloquently to convey his works essence to others." She continues:

"In his paintings, Sri Chinmoy lets his art flow from his heart in a pouring forth of creative energy. He expresses sentiments of harmony, oneness and childlike joy in his art. His art, abundant in the creative force, is ever effecting new inspiration, an inspiration for The Journey. He says: "My soul is a bird of fire, winging the infinite.""

"To be sure, the symbol of the bird figures prominently throughout his artistic expression, being a metaphor for the artistic expressions, being a metaphor for the aspiration of the Soul, or the Inner Self, to transcend itself,

Sri Chinmoy with one of his larger paintings

as it flies upward or expands outward into the skies of freedom and liberation; for much as the human life so inextricably essential to its very existence and evolution, so also the soul seeks its own liberation...

May the soul-bird within each one of us, fly to its own greatest heights." *Brochure: Jharna-Kala Fountain-Art. Jharna-Kala Foundation,* Parsons Blvd, NY. Courtesy Manifestation-Glow Press, Jamaica, Queens, NY.

Using a variety of sponges, brushes and even his own hand, Sri Chinmoy's artworks are a bold fusion of vibrant colours. He paints at a rapid, yet unhurried pace, doing so, he says, in a meditative consciousness. He does not use his mind but rather works spontaneously from within.

"These paintings come to me spontaneously," he says. "I see a streak of light and I follow it. When I paint, I do not have in mind how many I am going to do. No, I only try to become a perfect instrument of the Supreme by surrendering to His Will." *Meetings With Luminaries In The Philippines, (1993),* Agni Press.

A visit to an exhibition of Sri Chinmoy's paintings can be an extremely fulfilling meditative experience, as each painting has its own uniqueness, and has a capacity to absorb the viewer in the painting style, which is effortless and natural.

Sri Chinmoy's works of paintings and bird-drawings have been exhibited in Canada, Australia,

Jharna-Kala gallery function, 1992

America, England, New Zealand, Japan, Asia and in many prestigious galleries around the world. Most notably, they have been exhibited at the Carousel du Louvre, the Mall Gallery in London, the National Gallery in Ottawa   and the   Australian Parliament House in Canberra.

I was present at a gathering in downtown Ottawa, 1994, where more than one million soul-bird drawings were magnificently displayed and exhibited in a four- storey building. This was truly an astounding and monumental labour of love exhibited by the Master's students. Today, the legacy of Sri Chinmoy's artwork still continues to be felt, as his disciples display his work, utilising even mobile units in major cities around the world.

The United Nations

"The United Nations is the chosen instrument of God. To be a chosen instrument of God means to be a divine messenger carrying the Banner of God's inner Vision and Outer Manifestation. One day the world will not only treasure and cherish the soul of the United Nations, but also claim the soul of the United Nations as its very own with enormous pride, for this soul is all-loving, all-nourishing and all-fulfilling" *The Garland of Nations Souls, (1972),* Agni Press.

Sri Chinmoy was a frequent visitor to the United Nations. Indeed he regularly held prayerful meditations for delegates and staff twice weekly, for 37 years. Sri Chinmoy saw the UN, not merely as a political institution but as what he called "The Heart- Home of the World-Body." Sri Chinmoy's work at the UN was far removed from politics, but rather dedicated to bringing to the fore and nurturing the ideals of which it stood. Speaking of the UN, Sri Chinmoy says that it can teach us how to share, it can teach us:

"The message of trust, the message of concern, the message of unity in diversity and, finally, the message of universal peace." *(Ibid).*

According to Sri Chinmoy, the ideals of the UN are brotherhood, love, peace, soul- sharing, and universal oneness. He feels that in order to understand its significance, one needs to think in terms of a world body; in terms of 'we' and 'ours'. One needs to feel like Socrates, like a citizen of the world, rather than a separate entity. Sri Chinmoy gives us the lofty vision of the UN thus:

"The body of the United Nations is trying to serve humanity. The vital of the United Nations is striving to energise humanity. The mind of the

United Nations is longing to inspire humanity. The heart of the United Nations is crying to love humanity. Finally, the soul of the United Nations is flying to embrace humanity." *(Ibid).*

To Sri Chinmoy, the United Nations is not a dream, but a reality with sincere efforts being made by the people who work there. He feels that it is only by our joint efforts, that we can achieve what the Supreme wants in the world of aspiration and dedication. As our efforts intensify, so too will our world progress, and the UN will play a major part in this evolvement. The following prose shows the importance of this relationship:

> "To us, the United Nations is not a mere building, it is not a mere concept, and it is not wishful thinking or even a dream. It is a reality which is growing, glowing and manifesting its radiance here, there, all-where, throughout the length and breadth of the world. All those who are sincerely crying for a oneness-family, according to their receptivity, are receiving light from the soul of the United Nations." *The Inner Role of the United Nations,* Agni Press, 1993.

"The outer message of the United Nations is Peace. The inner message of the United Nations is Love. The inmost message of the United Nations is Oneness. Peace we feel. Love we become. Oneness we manifest." *The Tears of Nation- Hearts,* (1974), Agni Press.

Sri Chinmoy first went to the UN in 1970, at the invitation of the then UN Secretary General, U Thant. With his support, Sri Chinmoy began an inter-denominational meditation group at the United Nations. It is called: Sri Chinmoy: the Peace Meditations at the United Nations. Sri Chinmoy has done much to promote the ideals of religious tolerance and religious understanding, and has spoken at numerous interfaith events in diverse places. In 1993, he was invited to give the opening meditation at the Parliament of World Religions in Chicago, an honour which was repeated again in Barcelona in 2004. The Peace Meditations at the UN continues to this day. Its motto is:

> "We believe that each man has the potentiality of reaching the Ultimate Truth. We also believe that man cannot and will *not remain imperfect forever.* Each man is an instrument of God. When the hour strikes, each individual soul listens to the inner dictates of God. When man listens to God, his imperfections are turned into perfections, his ignorance into knowledge, his searching mind into revealing light and his uncertain reality into all-

fulfilling Divinity." *The Garland of Nations-Souls, Section 1, (1972),* Agni Press.

To perpetuate U Thant's memory, Sri Chinmoy created The U Thant Peace Award, to acknowledge and honour individuals or organisations for distinguished accomplishments, toward the attainment of world peace: First offered in 1982, the award is given to those who exemplify the lofty spiritual ideals of the late United Nations Secretary-General, and who implemented his ideals in this tireless pursuit.

Among the luminaries who have lovingly accepted the U Thant Peace Award from Sri Chinmoy, are His Holiness Pope John Paul II and five Nobel Laureates:

President Mikhail Gorbachev, President Nelson Mandela, Mother Teresa, Archbishop Desmond Tutu and the Dalai Lama, as well as former United Nations Secretaries-General Javier Perez de Cuellar and Kurt Waldheim. Daw Aye Aye Thant,

Sri Chinmoy and Pope John Paul 11. June 18th, 1980. The Vatican.

U Thant's daughter and President of the U Thant Institute, is also a recipient of this coveted Award. Secretary-General Perez de Cuellar has referred to Sri Chinmoy as 'the Soul of the United Nations.'

Sri Chinmoy and Pope Paul V1. March 22nd, 1972. The Vatican.

Sri Chinmoy and Archbishop Desmond Tutu.

In memory of Sri Chinmoy's Mahasamadhi, a most moving tribute and celebration of his life was held at the UN on the 30th October, 2007, in his honour. Present were many dignitaries, ambassadors, athletes, councilmen and leaders from six interfaith religious traditions. They included Pir Zia Inayat Khan, President of the Sufi Order International, and Maggid Yitzhak Buxbaum, the Director of the Jewish Spirit.

Above; From left to right.
Photo by Dhanu Alaimo. Courtesy of http://www.srichinmoybio.co.uk/news/celebration-life-sri-chinmoy. Last visited 15th June, 2012.

The Ven. Ashin Indaka, Chief Monk of the Mahasi Meditation Retreat Center Association; The Very Rev. James Parks Morton, Founder of the Interfaith Center of New York and Dean Emeritus of the Cathedral of St. John the Divine; Nana Boakyewa Yiadom I, Queen of Adamorobe, Aburi-Akuapem (Ghana); Swami Amarnathananda, Head Monk of the Bharat Sevashram Sangha of North America; Pir Zia Inayat-Khan, President of the Sufi Order International; Maggid Yitzhak Buxbaum, Director, Jewish Spirit; Let us conclude with the Master's sublime and profound dream of the United Nations:

> " ... The dream of the United Nations, the vision of the United Nations, the reality of the United Nations came from the Highest, The Absolute Highest. For the establishment of world peace, UN the temple, UN the shrine, UN the heart and UN the Soul are unparalleled. The United Nations is not a mere building. The United Nations is a reservoir of Divine Light for the manifestation of world peace. Then again, it can be something else altogether, if the instruments do not do the right thing, and do not want to become the right persons. If the instruments are unwilling, then what can the poor Inner Pilot of the United Nations do?" *Sri Chinmoy Answers, Part 8, (1997), (Cited in Disciples Companion, Vol 2, P. 178, Agni Press.).*

The Oneness-heart-tears and Smiles

The Oneness-Heart-Tears and Smiles project, is somewhat different from Sri Chinmoy's other manifestations, as it is solely based on supplying humanitarian aid to the needy in many countries around the world. Sri Chinmoy set up the programme in 1990, to assist one of his friends – Mikhail Gorbachev – President of the Soviet Union, who requested help with supplying aid to children suffering from leukaemia at a Hospital there. The programmes have now expanded to include Asia, Australia and New Zealand, North and South America, Africa and the Caribbean, as well as Europe.

The Oneness-Heart-Tears and Smiles deliver aid such as medical, surgical and pharmaceutical. They also obtain bicycles and computers, as well as lots of school material which is desperately needed in some areas of different countries. The Oneness-Heart-Tears and Smiles effort is a practical opportunity to build bridges between communities and nations.   It is also a golden opportunity to serve those who are less fortunate than others, and to instill hope.

One of the most popular initiatives is the "Kids to Kids" programme. This is a programme where school children collect personal and educational supplies for their counterparts in economically disadvantaged countries. This involves sending practical aid such as school supplies, and also toys, artwork and other creative children's work. By so doing, it reinforces the idea that humanitarian service is more than just the giving of material aid, but also creating a sense of oneness and friendship between different people of different countries.

All this fits well with Sri Chinmoy's teachings, as he has told us that we can only serve. Humanity is our brothers and sisters and so we strive to play, however small or large a part, in improving, enriching the lives of, and giving selflessly to the betterment of those in need.

Sri Chinmoy, the Founder of Oneness-Heart-Tears and Smiles, says of the programme:

> "Our humanitarian service is not our self-motivated, condescending act of charity to the poor and needy. It is a gigantic opportunity to feed, nourish and strengthen our own poor brothers and sisters so that they can, side by side, march along with us to proclaim the world-oneness-victory of God the Creation." - Sri Chinmoy.

The work of Oneness-Heart Tears and Smiles continues today, whether by responding to Tsunami's in Japan or an earthquake or tornado someplace else. It is made up of a global network of medical and health professionals, private volunteers and concerned individuals on five continents. They are dedicated to alleviating the plight of suffering humanity, and to providing essential supplies and services to needy and disadvantaged people of the world, wherever they may be.

Working closely with other aid agencies, governments, local NGO's, national leaders, community groups and corporations, the Oneness-Heart-Tears and Smiles obtains and distributes humanitarian supplies in programmes that respond to disaster relief requests, health and education needs and regional development projects.

These endeavours of the OHTS are carried out by members of the international Sri Chinmoy Centres. There are no political, religious or corporate affiliations, and it is entirely staffed by volunteers who organise the collection, storage, transportation and distribution of all materials to their worldwide destinations.

Sri Chinmoy International Peace-blossoms

In 1986, a Sri Chinmoy Peace Bridge was inaugurated in Rhode Island, USA. Not long afterwards, the Sri Chinmoy London Centre – of which I am a member – inaugurated a Sri Chinmoy Peace Mile at Battersea Park. This was done in conjunction with the then Greater London Council, and was initiated by our London Meditation Centre Leader called Bhavani. These two projects were perhaps the pioneers for the Sri Chinmoy International Peace-Blossom Projects, which were to follow in 1989.

A Sri Chinmoy Peace Blossom

Sri Chinmoy himself came to the inauguration of the Sri Chinmoy Peace Mile at Battersea Park. He was followed by many disciples from around Europe and also some from other countries who were very inspired by the

Sri Chinmoy Peace Airport, Philippines, 1993.

very idea of a Peace Mile in Sri Chinmoy's name. Of course they also wanted to be with their Teacher. Since that time, over a thousand Peace Blossoms have sprung up in major cities, and countries around the world. They range from plaques at airports, mountains, monuments, world famous waterfalls such as Niagara Falls in Canada, and Victoria Falls in Zimbabwe, to Sri Chinmoy Peace Capitals, Sri Chinmoy Streets and Airports, to even countries dedicated to peace.

There are also Sri Chinmoy Bridges, Sri Chinmoy Peace Trees and an Eternal Peace Flame at Honnorbryggen, Aker Brygge Port, Oslo, Norway.

They serve to inspire, promote a world of peace and harmony, and to perpetuate humanity's com-mon dream of a Oneness-World. Each Peace-Blossom is established through the auspices of the governing local, state or national officials, and many are marked with an ins-pirational plaque generally unveiled at the ceremony of Sri Chinmoy students, dignitaries and the general public.

Sri Chinmoy Peace Blossom, Canberra, Australia, 1995.

Eternal Peace Flame Installation

The Eternal peace flame was dedicated in 2001 by Sri Chinmoy. This temporary installation was witnessed by more than 1500 persons including Ambassadors, National Politicians, Luminaries and Athletes. It was temporarily installed at the Pier of Honor on Oslo harbour.

In 2002, the Eternal Peace Flame was installed permanently at Aker Brygge, a complex on the Oslo Harbor frequented by hundreds of thousands of people each year. A landmark on the port, the Eternal Peace Flame burns brightly and serves as a beacon of light and inspiration.

The Eternal Peace Flame at Twilight

The Eternal Peace Flame was initially installed as a temporary donation to the city of Oslo from Sri Chinmoy. The original location was at the Pier of Honor, which is the pier of the King of Norway. This unique location had a 180 degree view of Oslo's magnificent harbor.

The Eternal Peace Flame at Dawn

The Eternal Peace Flame was visited at its original location by thousands of people each day. A special registry was affixed to the flame's base in which hundreds of people from dozens of nation expressed through word their aspiration for peace. A number of persons voiced their most resounding appreciation of Oslo for displaying a piece of art as inspiring as the Eternal Peace Flame.

The Flame Burns Bright in All Seasons

The Eternal Peace Flame is a striking engineering marvel with numerous state-of- the-art controls enabling it to stay alight even during the most inclement weather. Here the Flame is pictured during a normal Norwegian winter's day.

Sri Chinmoy Visits the Flame

In 2003, Sri Chinmoy visited the Flame at its new location at Aker Brygge for the first time. He gave an inspired impromptu concert at the Flame on his flute which happened to be with him in his car.

Statue of Sri Chinmoy Unveiled at Eternal Peace Flame

The Statue of Sri Chinmoy was unveiled at a ceremony on 27th October, 2008.
Courtesy of *www.eternalpeaceflame.org/about*. *Last visited 4th August, 2012.*

Since the Master's Mahasamadhi on the 11th October, 2007, there have been significant efforts to have his sculptured Statue, placed in key locations around the world. This has been quite successful, and the first inauguration was at the Aker Brygge Port, Oslo, Norway, adjacent to and overlooking the Eternal Peace Flame. The Statue was inaugurated with an inter-denominational cere-mony on October 27th,

Sri Chinmoy Peace Statue, Nepal.

2008. To date there are thirteen Sri Chinmoy Statues in nearly as many countries, with quite a few more in the pipeline for the near and distant future.

Sri Chinmoy World Peace-Dreamer Statue, Vienna

Sri Chinmoy Peace Statue, Mazatland, Mexico

Speaking of the Statue, Sri Chinmoy says:

> "When they see the statue like this (folding his hands), they will see that aspiration and compassion go together. I am aspiring for Heaven to descend; and when I receive something, I am offering it to mankind. I am aspiring, I am going up, and I am receiving from Above. Then, from Heaven I am bringing down compassion, and that compassion I am offering to mankind. Inside that compassion there will be light and power."
> *(Taken from the Brochure of Shilpataru, a sculptor and disciple for whom the Master posed on August 15th, 2000.)*

Since that time, the London sculptor Kaivalya Torpy – also a disciple of the Master - has moulded Sri Chinmoy Statues to include Sri Chinmoy holding our World Harmony Torch. There have also been a walking Statue and bust done by Asidhari Damon Burns, and plans are being worked on for sitting and reclining statues also. I have been present at the Welsh, Prague and Oslo Statues, noticed the love and reverence shown them, sometimes by people who are complete strangers. They walk by, see something in the Statue and stop. They touch, hold, take pictures and pay their respects before moving on to their destinations.

Kaivalya, The Sculptor, with the Sri Chinmoy World Harmony Peace Statue, Wales.

To commemorate the London Olympics, A Sri Chinmoy Peace Dreamer Statue was specially made by Kaivalya Torpy and displayed at University College, London, an Olympic Venue, on Saturday the 28th July, 2012.

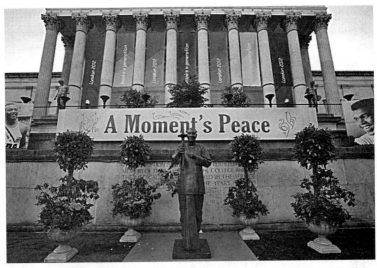

The Sri Chinmoy World Peace Dreamer Statue, UCL, London, UK.

It shows Sri Chinmoy offering the World Harmony/Sri Chinmoy Oneness-Home Peace Torch with his right hand, and his left folded across his chest in supplication. This Statue was commissioned by three Olympians: Sudahota Carl Lewis, winner of nine Olympic medals, Tatyana Lebedeva, winner of five Olympic Medals, and Tegla Loroupe, Olympian and marathon champion.

Baroness Shreela Flather, Tegla La Roupe, Sudahota Carl Lewis and Bob Beamon

This magnificent sculpture was to be offered to Boris Johnson, Mayor of London, as a gift to the City of London. Unfortunately the Mayor could not be there, and so Baroness Shreela Flather, Professor Michael Worton, Vice-Provost of University College, London, and the Borough Mayors who were present at the ceremony, were all invited to unveil and receive the Statue, on behalf of the City of London. The wonderful and memorable Ceremony was aptly called *A Moment's Peace. (www.amomentspeace2012.com)*. Last visited 10th September, 2012.

Devashishu Torpy, Master of ceremonies, addressing the audience

The Christmas Trip

Towards the end of every year, Sri Chinmoy used to travel abroad with about 200 – 400 of his students for a spiritual sojourn. At its high point there were 1,300 disciples who were able to join a portion of the Trip. They were able to join at some point for a week or so, during the duration of the three months. He did not like the cold of western winters, but he also utilised the trip as a way of responding to the needs of the Soul of the individual country, which he sometimes said had requested him to visit. Sri Chinmoy also said that his students made tremendous spiritual progress when they were on this 'spiritual journey' and encouraged them to come whenever they could. Here are a couple of examples:

"Some of you make unimaginable progress during the Christmas trip. That is why I beg people to come. Right from the beginning, spirituality is a matter of faith"

"The Christmas Trip is the golden opportunity for the disciples to make progress. Every day is an opportunity, but the Christmas Trip is a golden opportunity. Happiness is progress and progress is happiness. The happiness that people get on the Christmas Trip is innocent happiness. Innocent happiness embodies true cheerfulness. Here people are moving around looking at things, and going on excursions. This is all innocent happiness. Innocent happiness and progress will always go together" *Sri Chinmoy Answers, Part 26, Section 1, (2000)* Agni Press.

Sri Chinmoy spoke of the disciple as giving new light and receiving new light on such trips. On the material plane, the disciple gives his money-power, which benefits hundreds of local stores. On the inner plane, the disciple gives his soul-power. This is done through the disciple's prayer-life and meditation-life. By virtue of these regular daily spiritual practices, the people of the country will see something in the faces or eyes of the disciples, which they may not see elsewhere. (*Sri Chinmoy Answers, Part 6, (1995)*, Agni Press).

Certainly we as disciples played many games, had innocent fun, shopped a lot, and engaged in prayerful silence and meditation on a daily basis.

During such trips, Sri Chinmoy would meet with Presidents, Kings, Government officials, Elders, other dignitaries, luminaries and various sportsmen and women. Some would express a need to meet him, but generally these meetings were put together by students of Sri Chinmoy at his requests. It gave our Guru the opportunity to share with many men and women, in which they were generally inspired by him, by us disciples, by our Guru's light manifesting in and through us. Sri Chinmoy also spoke of giving something to those who were able to receive inwardly. This he did through music concerts, art exhibitions, public plays, gifts and so forth. He taught mostly in silence, and conveyed his love through his sublime, blessed, contemplative and compassionate smile

It was mostly a smaller gathering during these trips, and so both Master and students had time to meet together in a more intimate way: There were lots of morning, afternoon and evening functions, which were generally organised in the Hotel in which the Master stayed. There was also time for sight-seeing, shopping, visiting the beach and some more adventurous undertakings such as trekking, surfing and so forth, by those who felt inclined. These trips were fondly called 'The Christmas Trip,' by Sri Chinmoy and his students, and would normally happen between November and February the following year, lasting initially one but later up to three months.

In many ways these trips were like a working holiday for the Master. He never wasted a moment and was always fond of attending to the needs of his disciples, or drawing, writing, weight-lifting, singing, teaching songs and so forth. True, he would sometimes go for a walk or run around the perimeter of the Hotel where we all stayed. At other times he drove his little car, and as he became more senior in age, he rode his scooter also. As in New York, it did not take disciples long to figure out what he was doing and the crowd would generally gather to hear the 'juicy' stories of the Master's childhood, jokes, questions and answers or just general conversations.

Just as mornings were taken up with prayers and meditations, so too the evenings had lots of plays and performances. Sometimes we had invited guests at functions and these added all the more to the inspiration and prayerful atmosphere of the place. There was also lots of laughter and innocent fun. Sri Chinmoy would compose various songs and the excellent girl and boy singers would teach them to us all.

We had singing daily as well as group performances of stories, musical and vocal groups and lots of plays. The Master had a way of telling some stories which were then written down into play form and performed on stage by the disciples later on. I recall acting out one such play given to me by Sri Chinmoy, during which time I had only a few days to gather some boys together, and then rehearse. It was a funny story called: *Even God is not allowed to go to Church*. In that play, the priest had turned God away because He was neither rich nor intelligent. I must have done well, as the group got loud applause at the end, and my Guru praised me highly and gave me extra *Prasad*.

Mango Prasad

Of course the Master did not always stay indoors. He would sometimes go out, either to see official guests, shopping, boat-riding or just looking around. I loved the boat-rides very much. Generally we would all gather around Sri Chinmoy and he would chat, tell funny stories, or make individual comments to disciples which would make us all laugh. Mostly he wrote poems or aphorisms, drew birds or taught songs. Sri Chinmoy would compose the song there and then, the girl and boy musicians would sing it once or twice, and then we would all follow. The songs may have seemed difficult in the beginning but within five minutes we were usually all singing with great cheerfulness and joy.

This was the Master's way of teaching songs and sometimes reciting aphorisms. He did these for many years and it was not often that he came prepared with songs for us to sing, especially on the Christmas Trip. Sometimes he would compose hundreds of poems there. Our rehearsals and performances were always followed by *Prasad* which included sweets which the Master would occasionally throw to us with a large grin. We as disciples loved this very much.

Today, just over four years after the Masters' Mahasamadhi, the tradition of the Christmas Trip continues. It is adeptly put together by Alo Devi, Savyasachi and Saraswati, the latter two, both long-standing disciples of Sri Chinmoy. They were instrumental and luminous lights right from the very beginning, all the way from Puerto Rico in the mid sixties. While Sri Chinmoy is not in the physical any more, we know that he is still there watching over us, as we pray, sing, have laughter and innocent fun, and continue his work of meeting with significant people, for the manifestation of his mission: of loving and serving God, the Supreme, in and through humanity.

Conclusion

Sri Chinmoy's disciples have been busy in many other areas. One of the most frequent is the giving of Meditation classes free of charge, as taught and encouraged by the Master. Indeed all his offerings were free. Some of Sri Chinmoy's students are experienced class-givers, and they travel to other countries at the request of their friends and also seekers, to give classes on the meditative life. This is a most soulful contribution to the community, in so far as it inspires them to live more peaceful lives. Some of them also organise Peace-festivals and use music and drama to encourage harmony and goodwill to all.

Finally, one other way of looking at Sri Chinmoy's legacy is to see and feel the direct impact it has upon fellow Sri Chinmoy students as well as me. I am always moved and deeply touched to see so many disciples, still gathering in New York for the Master's arrival in the West celebrations, (April 13th, 1964), and his birthday Celebrations (August 27th, 1931). There is also a small but transcendent celebration for his Mahasamadhi on October 11th, 2007. Almost five years after his passing, all the routine and programmes still continue. From the light performances of skits, circus, story-telling and jokes, to the more soulful prayers and meditations, excellent musical performances, videos, races and 'walk-by' meditations.

The 'walk-by' meditations are still done the way the Master taught us. We do them in rows of three's or four's walking with folded hands prayerfully towards the Master's Aspiration-Temple-shrine. There is usually Sri Chinmoy's meditative music playing in the background as we go past the Temple-shrine, offering incense or flowers as a token of our love and devotion. Then there is the more sweetly organised way of walk-by, again taught to us by the Master.

Here the disciple walks towards the sacred shrine, turns right, walks some 25 metres to the other end, then turns left and repeat the walk. This continues until the lead disciple is at the other end of the Aspiration-Ground and many more disciples are accommodated in the process. This facilitates ease and greater numbers at the Aspiration ground. It also instils a deep sense of reverence.

Sri Chinmoy's outer outpourings and that of the disciples endure and have even expanded. While the Master continues to be missed, no doubt, in some ways it can be an insult to dwell on this, as the Master's presence and guidance is still so incredibly strong in all we do! So yes, all these legacies are necessary to inspire, encourage and guide us and others, but perhaps our Guruji's inner presence inside our hearts is by far the best. Here are two stories to re-enforce this statement.

One quiet night, about 21:45 hrs, I was taking a chapter of my manuscript to a friend about a mile from my house. It was not long before I heard a loud shout behind me and turned around. I then noticed a young man, about twenty one years old approaching me. He was about thirty metres away and was shouting at me.

"Why are you looking at me?" He said, and kept on shouting and repeating his question as he got closer. He did not seem drunk, but his face was threatening and frightening. I immediately began to apologise even though I had not initially seen him. Indeed, I was facing forward, and he came from behind. As he got to within six feet of me, he pushed his hand in his pocket and I felt a sense of impending doom.

I immediately remembered that Sri Chinmoy had asked us to chant "Supreme" quite quickly if ever we are faced with danger. Folding my hands right there in the street, and looking up towards Heaven, I began to chant powerfully and faithfully, abandoning my focus on the young man who was about to attack me. When I eventually looked in his direction some 30 seconds later, he was looking at me strangely and walking backwards away from me. I heard a voice call, and he turned around and walked away.

Here's a more positive and sublime experience. One silent morning, some three years after the Master's Mahasamadhi, I was in a deep sleep at home in London, when my Spirit seemed to ascend to a very high plane. I found myself sitting at the feet of the Master with some other disciples. After some divine chat, the Master got up and started to leave. He had gone only three feet or so when he turned around, gave me a most loving smile, and came slowly back. Placing his hand on my head, he gave me what is perhaps the most powerful experience that I have had to date.

Surely the Master is with us. More than his legacy, his infinite and eternal spirit continues on this, his eternal journey, and, as reported by so many disciples, is frequently felt during our earthly sojourn.

– Manatita 7th May, 2012.

CHAPTER SIXTEEN

A Selection of Sri Chinmoy's Lofty Utterances on Duty, Action and Selfless Work

"Each self-giving action of mine
Immediately becomes
A most beautiful flower
In my Lord's Victory Garland"

My Christmas-New Year Vacation-Aspiration-Prayers, Part 32, (2005), Agni Press

"Not word, but work:
This sweet message awakens strength
In our Heart.
Inside work remains hidden
The fragrance of flowers.
Let work be the language of our heart.
Our only aim is progress
Not victory or failure."

The Garland Of Love-Light, (1973), Agni Press,

"A spiritual person has found his work. His work is dedicated action. Indeed, he has no need of any other blessedness. His action is the divine acceptance of earthly existence. And for this he needs a perfect body, a strong mind, a soulful heart and a supremely inspired life of inner receptivity and outer capacity." *Philosopher-Thinkers: The Power-Towers Of The Mind And Poet-Seers: The Fragrance-Hours Of The Heart In The West,* 1998, Agni Press,

"Whenever we work, we can and should feel that we are working for God. Right now when you are working, you may not think of God, or you may not feel the reality of God. You see physical work as just work. But if you can see work as an opportunity to express your capacity, or to reveal your goodness, your divinity, then most certainly you are working for God at that time. By working, or serving, you have to feel that you are moving toward your goal"

"If you are a labourer and are working with your hands, your mind can be inside God, your heart can be inside God, and you can consciously place your very action inside God." *Fifty Freedom-Boats To One Golden Shore, Part 4,* (1974) Agni Press.

"There are some spiritual Masters who allow their disciples to live vagabond lives. Our path is not like that. I ask my disciples to either work or study. If you work, if you earn a decent, modest living and if you lead a normal life, I will be very happy. It is absolutely necessary to lead a normal life"

"You have to feel that work, if you do it devotedly, is the prayer of the body. The body's prayer is necessary, absolutely necessary, to please God. As the heart prays, the mind, the vital and the body also have to pray. When we say that the body has to pray, we have to know that this prayer is done only through selfless service." *Service-Boat And Love-Boatman, Part 1,* (1974) Agni Press.

"Work, when it is done in a divine spirit and for a divine purpose, is dedicated service. The combination of meditation and dedicated service makes a man perfect." *Fifty Freedom-Boats To One Golden Shore, Part 2, (1974),* Agni Press.

"Wherever your Lord Supreme
Asks you to work, That particular place Should be Heaven to you."
Ten Thousand Flower-Flames, Part 92, (1983), Agni Press.

"You get joy when I ask you to do something for me, to work for me. I get joy if I ask you to work for me and also if I ask you not to work. It is the same with the spiritual Masters. The Supreme asks some souls to work for Him on earth and some not to. Some souls, when they realise God, don't want to manifest Divinity on earth and with God's approval, they remain in the soul's region. But those who want to manifest are like divine soldiers. They come down again and again and work for the Supreme for the transformation of humanity. For these souls, manifestation is always necessary. They feel that if manifestation doesn't take place, then realisation is useless." *God, Avatars And Yogis, (1977),* Agni Press.

"If you offer your good will, or if you have a very high, sublime meditation, then on the inner plane you are executing the Will of the Supreme. Undoubtedly, that is also selfless service. Anything that you do to become soulfully one, devotedly one, unreservedly one, unconditionally one with the Will of the Supreme is selfless service." *Service-Heroes, (1978),* Agni Press.

"God has to occupy one's mind; and in this state of divine concentration, one should serve humanity. At that very hour, service itself becomes the greatest reward. Although meditation and service constitute totally different approaches in the field of spirituality, work and dedicated service are nothing short of pure meditation." *Commentary On The Bhagavad Gita,* (1971), Agni Press.

"Service can do many things for us. First of all, we should know that service done in a divine spirit is the greatest opportunity that we have in our possession to kill our pride and vanity and to obliterate the stamp of ego. It is in dedicated service that we see the universal harmony, we grow into the universal consciousness." *The Garden of Love-light, (1973),* Agni Press

"Karma Yoga is desireless action undertaken for the sake of the Supreme. *Karma Yoga* is man's genuine acceptance of his earthly existence. *Karma Yoga* is man's dauntless march across the battlefield of life.

Karma Yoga does not see eye to eye with those who hold that the activities of human life are of no importance. *Karma Yoga* claims that life is a divine opportunity for serving God. This particular Yoga is not only the Yoga of physical action; it includes the aspirant's moral and inner life as well." *Yoga And The Spiritual Life. The Journey of India's Soul, (1971),* Agni Press.

"Action itself does not have a binding power; neither does it need one. It is the desire in action that has the power to bind us and tell us that freedom is not for mortals. But if, in action, sacrifice looms large, or if action is done in a spirit of sacrifice, or if action is considered another name for sacrifice, then action is perfection, action is illumination, action is liberation

From action, action springs. Action as such can never put an end to action. Action is continuous. Action is perpetual. No matter how hard we work, how long we work; mere action can never show us the Face of the Supreme. He is a true Karma-Yogi who works for the Supreme and for the Supreme alone." *Commentary On The Bhagavad Gita, (1971),* Agni Press.

"Action is entering into the battlefield of life. Action is conquering life's untold miseries and teeming limitations. Action is transforming life's devouring imperfection into glowing perfection. Action is something infinitely deeper and higher than the mere survival of physical existence. Action is the secret supreme, which enables us to enter into the Life Eternal." *Eastern Light For The Western Mind, (1973),* Agni Press

"For him who is embodied, action is a necessity, action is a must. Man is the result of a divine sacrifice. It is sacrifice that can vision the truth and fulfil man's existence All beings must follow their nature. No escape there is, nor can there be. What can restraint do? Man's duty is Heaven's peerless blessing. One must know what one's duty is. Once duty is known, it is to be performed to the last."

"Life's duty, performed with a spontaneous flow of self-offering to humanity under the express guidance of the inner being, can alone transform life into Beauty, the heavenly Beauty of the world within, and earthly Beauty of the world without." *Commentary On The Bhagavad Gita,* (1971) Agni Press.

"Poetry that springs from a devout heart leads kindred hearts to the ever-sweet One and makes of them a Republic with Him for President. No other divine faculty perhaps has a greater power of transcendence over limits to the illimitable. In the bright days that are dawning upon the earth well may we look for the leaven of transcendental poetry, to uplift the whole human mass.

The poet has the divine faith, the inner intuition that the existence of the One Supreme Divine has hardly anything to do with the commonly sought spiritual experience side-by-side with common miseries. In order to write a poem, the poet must transport himself to the sphere of the Muse and lose himself there. He has to be like a flame that burns away everything but itself." *Philosopher-Thinkers: The Power-Towers Of The Mind And Poet-Seers: The Fragrance-Hours Of The Heart In The West, (1998),* Agni Press.

This is a unique example:

The Absolute

No mind, no form, I only exist:
Now ceased all will and thought.
The final end of Nature's dance,
I am it whom I have sought.

A realm of Bliss bare, ultimate:
Beyond both knower and known;
A rest immense I enjoy at last,
I face the One alone.

I have crossed the secret ways of life:
I have become the Goal.
The Truth immutable is revealed;
I am the way, the God-Soul.

My spirit aware of all the heights,
I am mute in the core of the Sun.
I barter nothing with time and deeds.
My cosmic play is done.
Sri Chinmoy, My Flute, (1972) Agni Press.

Salutations To My Guru

Bhagavan Sri Chinmoy:
Avatar of the era;
Yogi of the highest magnitude;
Sovereign of the Eternal Now.
I bow to You in deep reverence.

Bhagavan Sri Chinmoy:
God of Gods.
Thou who art not the body,
But the manifestation, of a divine power on Earth.
Oh God-man of the ever-transcending beyond.
I bow to You in deep reverence.

Bhagavan Sri Chinmoy:
Mother, Father, Friend and Advocate.
You came to the West in 1964.
At the command of Your Beloved Lord Supreme.
You taught: The Spirituality of the East,
and the dynamism of the West must go together;
That Matter has to be
the conscious expression of the Spirit.
I bow to you in deep reverence.

Bhagavan Sri Chinmoy:
Seer-athlete; poet; artist; musician; weightlifter supreme!
Writer of over 1500 books!
Composer of over 22,000 devotional songs!
Painter of over 150,000 paintings!
Lifter of over 7000lbs with either hand!
Creator of Soul-birds, Peace-Blossoms, Oneness-Home
Peace Runs, World Harmony Runs and Eternal Flames,
I bow to You in deep reverence.

Bhagavan Sri Chinmoy:
You taught the ideal of Self-transcendence.......
Going beyond, beyond, into the ever-transcending beyond......
Love, Devotion and Surrender incarnate.
You placed everything,

At the feet of Your Beloved Lord Supreme, saying:
"In My case, everything is 100% God's Grace and
God's compassion."
I bow to You in deep reverence.

Oh Mother India, land of Himalayan Souls.
Birthplace of Yoga Maya and Shashi Kumar Ghose,
Parents of 'Madal' Chinmoy Kumar Ghose,
Seventh and final child, born August 27th 1931;
Attained Mahasamadhi October 11th, 2007,
I bow to you in deep reverence.

1992. Revised Oct 25, 2007 – Manatita.

Glossary

Page IV

1. 'Supreme.' Sri Chinmoy was very fond of this word and it was his favourite word for God. Sri Chinmoy gives his reasons in Chapter 11 (Love, Devotion And Surrender .....)

Prologue Part One.

1. Aspiration-Ground is the sanctuary where Sri Chinmoy and his disciples met. This enclave is tucked away beneath some over-hanging trees at the back of a few houses in Jamaica, Queens, New York.

    Originally a tennis court, it was used by the Master and his disciples for spiritual practices and included tennis, which Guruji enjoyed playing for many years. He had a small hut (Gazebo) at the Southern end of the court.

    At the South-Westerly end of the Gazebo is a small track that the Master used for practising athletics and weight-lifting. To the North of this, was a somewhat untidy hollow area which was subsequently filled with earth and grass and progressively became a wonderful garden with time.

    The word *Aspiration* has been covered in greater detail in the book. Basically Sri Chinmoy used it to convey the meaning of a deeper cry or yearning within the seeker's heart, for Something Higher – a deep flame burning inside the seeker's heart for his/her beloved Self or God.

    Today the Aspiration-Ground is a pinnacle of beauty, Light and loftiness. With its overhanging trees, numerous pots and plants, and a beautiful Temple- Shrine at the northern end which has long since replaced the Gazebo. It was there that Guruji mostly stayed while we were attending functions or spiritual practices. A wonderful glimpse of Aspiration-Ground is given in the Epilogue of this book.

1. Aspiration-Temple. A beautifully designed Japanese styled sacred Temple, where the Master mostly stayed while he was with us at celebrations (twice yearly prayerful functions), and also at other times. It was always used for God-centred events.

Prologue Part Two

1. *What is the meaning of AUM?*

"AUM is a syllable that has a special significance and a creative power. AUM is the Mother of all mantras. When we chant AUM, what actually happens is that we bring down peace and light from above and create a universal harmony within and without us. When we repeat AUM, both our inner and outer beings become inspired and surcharged with a divine feeling and aspiration.

AUM has no equal. AUM has infinite power. Just by repeating AUM, we can realize God.

When you repeat AUM, please try to observe what actually happens. If you repeat the name of a cat, a dog or a monkey, or even of an ordinary person, you get no inspiration. But when you utter AUM, which is the symbol of the Creator, the life- breath of the Creator, you immediately get an inner feeling, the feeling that inspires your inner and outer movements to enlarge your vision and fulfil your life here on earth. This is the secret of AUM. If you want to cherish a secret all your life, then here is the secret. Please chant AUM and everything will be yours. The sound of AUM is unique. Generally we hear a sound when two things are struck together.

But AUM needs no such action. It is anahata, or unstruck; it is the soundless sound. A Yogi or spiritual Master can hear AUM self-generated in the inmost recesses of his heart. There are many ways to chant AUM. When you chant it loudly, you feel the omnipotence of the Supreme. When you chant it softly, you feel the delight of the Supreme. When you chant it silently, you feel the peace of the Supreme.

The universal AUM put forth by the Supreme is an infinite ocean. The individual AUM chanted by man is a drop in that ocean, but it cannot be separated from the ocean, and it can claim the infinite ocean as its very own. When one chants AUM out loud, one touches and calls forth the cosmic vibration of the supreme Sound.

It is best to chant Aum out loud, so its sound can vibrate even in your physical ears and permeate your entire body. This will convince your outer mind and give you a greater sense of joy and achievement. When chanting out loud, the "M" sound should last at least three times as long as the "AU" sound." – Sri Chinmoy. Courtesy of http://www. srichinmoy.org/resources/library/questions_answers/aum/ Last visited 24th June, 2012.

1b. Alo Devi is the most long-standing person in the Sri Chinmoy Centre Church, and has been with Guruji since the very beginning. Canadian by birth, her search for God led her to the Sri Aurobindo Ashram in Pondicherry, India, where she met Sri Chinmoy. Alo Devi was very instrumental in helping Sri Chinmoy to establish his mission in the West in the early days, and has continued to serve the mission up to this present moment.

> Ably assisted by Savyasachi and Saraswati, two devotional 'boy and girl' disciples, and who have been travelling with her from the beginning, she is well known as one of the luminary lights and major force behind activities such as our annual 'Christmas Trip' and classical concerts in New York.

2. Transcendental. The Transcendental is a photograph of Sri Chinmoy taken in an extremely high state of spiritual consciousness, called Samadhi in Yoga philosophy. It is used by disciples all around the world as the central means to facilitate their meditation and to invoke their own transcendental consciousness. It is generally carried on their person.

3. Ranjana Ghose is the Curator of the Jharna Kala Art Gallery and Pilgrim Museum in New York. She came to the Master quite young, and has been on Sri Chinmoy's Path over forty years.

An accomplished harmonium player, Ranjana is the leader of the Sri Chinmoy Bhajan Singers – a group created by Sri Chinmoy. They travel internationally, performing their sublime and soul-stirring *Bhajans* to disciples, seekers and devotees all over the world.

Ranjana has a remarkable eye and vision for all things artistic and aesthetically beautiful, and has been an invaluable pillar in the organisation and arrangement of Aspiration-Ground, Pilgrim-Museum and The Jharna Kala Art Foundation. She was also resourceful in the establishment of the Sri Chinmoy Bhajan Singers group, and in many other initiatives of the Sri Chinmoy Centre Church.

Chapter One

1.   Ashrita Furman is one of the earlier disciples of the Master. He conveyed reports, messages, questions and answers from disciples, national and international to and from the Master. Well known and well liked, Ashrita is a daring and dauntless spiritual soldier on the Master's Path. Ashrita holds the record for the most Guinness Records. (Well over one hundred). He is currently still breaking records, and has appeared on many T.V. shows and documentaries around the world.

Chapter Five

1.   'Boys and girls.' Sri Chinmoy used this term to address us a lot and we still do as his disciples. In fact he used a lot of pet names or terms, all significant in their own ways. There is the 'little' children's' group; 'big children' or simply 'children's' group; 'boys' group and 'girls' group. Singers were also in 'good' singers group; 'excellent' or 'super-excellent' singers group, and there was even a 'bad' singers group. Bad singers generally got better with practice and were also singled out for praise from the Master according to their performances and capacities.

Chapter Fourteen

Shurer Dhara was founded in the mid 1990's by Rezwana Choudhury Bannya who is an accomplished exponent of Rabindra Sangeet and an Associate Professor of the Faculty of Music and Drama Department, University of Dhaka. A distinguished alumna of Visva-Bharati in Santiniketan, the renowned Indian university founded by Rabindranath Tagore, she was inspired by her guru, Sreemati Kanika Bandopadhaye, a direct disciple of Tagore to continue the tradition of Santiniketan in Bangladesh.

The school was modelled after Tagore's vision on learning and child-rearing adapted to the needs of the 21st century which makes it imperative to keep the arts in education because they instill in students the habits of mind that lasts a life time. It promotes the idea that early musical training helps develop faculty for learning language and reasoning. *Adapted from http://shurer dhara.org. Last visited 10th June, 2012;* **http://simple.wikipedia.org/wiki/ Rabindranath_Tagore.** *Last visited 10th June, 2012.*

NOTE: "Sri" as it is used in this book, is not simply a title of reverence or that referred to a Swami, or even "Sir". It is generally used to refer to an illumined Soul, one who has achieved a conscious, irreversible and ceaseless oneness with God. The God- men, particularly of Sri Chinmoy's calibre, are believed by the disciple to be a direct descent of God in human form. (Avatar). Consequently the term "Sri", as it is used in this book, is more in keeping with "Lord", as Lord Rama, Lord Krishna, Lord Buddha, Lord Christ, Lord Chaitanya and others.

Bibliography

Bennett, Meredith Vidagdha. (1991) *Simplicity and Power: The Poetry of Sri Chinmoy*, Agni Press, Jamaica, Queens, New York.

Chetanananda, Swami. (1997), *God Lived With Them, p. 37*, Vedanta Society of St. Louis, Missouri, USA.

Ghose, Chinmoy Kumar (Sri Chinmoy). (1970) *My Rose Petals, p. 18; pp. 42-43*, Agni Press, Jamaica, Queens.

--- (1971) My *Rose-Petals, Part 1*, Agni Press, Jamaica, Queens, New York.

--- (1971) Yoga *And The Spiritual Life. The Journey of India's Soul, Section 1, Agni* Press, Jamaica, Queens, New York.

--- (1971) Songs *Of The Soul, p. 35, 54*, Agni Press, Jamaica, Queens, New York.

--- (1971) Commentary *On The Bhagavad Gita, Agni* Press, Jamaica, Queens, New York.

--- (1972) Eternity's *Breath, p.105, 107*, Agni Press, Jamaica, Queens, New York.

--- (1972) Arise, *Awake: Thoughts Of A Yogi*, Agni Press, Jamaica, Queens, New York.

--- (1972) The *Garland of Nations-Souls, Section 1, Agni Press, Jamaica, Queens, New York*.

--- (1972) Sri *Chinmoy, My Flute*, Agni Press, Jamaica, Queens, New York.

--- (1973) The *Son, Scene 2, Agni Press, Jamaica, Queens, New York*.

--- (1973) God's *Hour*, Agni Press, Jamaica, Queens, New York. (Ibid).

--- (1973) *America in Her Depts.* Agni Press, Jamaica, Queens, New York.

--- (1973) *Kennedy: The Universal Heart.* Agni Press, Jamaica, Queens, New York.

--- (1973) *The Garland of Love-Light*, Agni Press, Jamaica, Queens, New York.

--- (1973) *Eastern Light For The Western Mind.* Agni Press, Jamaica, Queens, New York.

--- (1974) T*he Vision of God's Dawn*, Agni Press, Jamaica, Queens, New York.

--- (1974) *Fifty Freedom-Boats To One Golden Shore, Part 4,* Agni Press, Jamaica, Queens, New York.

--- (1974) Earth's *Cry Meets Heaven's Smile, Part 2, Section 1,* Agni Press, Jamaica, Queens, New York.

--- (1974) *A God-Lover's Earth-Heaven- Life, Part 3,* Agni Press, Jamaica, Queens, New York.

---. (1974) *Canada Aspires, Canada Receives, Canada Achieves, Part 2,* Agni Press, Jamaica, Queens, New York.

---. (1974) *The Golden Boat, part 7.* Agni Press, Jamaica, Queens, New York.

---. (1974) *Cry Within: Yours Is The Goal,* Agni Press, Jamaica, Queens, New York.

---. (1974) *My Rose Petals, Part 1V,* Agni Press, Jamaica, Queens, New York.

---. (1974) A *Galaxy of Beautiful Stars.* Agni Press, Jamaica, Queens, New York.

--- (1974) The *Outer Runner And The Inner Running.* Agni Press, Jamaica, Queens, New York.

--- (1974) *Fifty Freedom-Boats To One Golden Shore, Part 2.* Agni Press, Jamaica, Queens, New York.

--- (1974) *Fifty Freedom-Boats To One Golden Shore, Part 4,* Agni Press, Jamaica, Queens, New York.

--- (1974) *Service-Boat And Love-Boatman.* Agni Press, Jamaica, Queens, New York.

--- (1975) Eternity's *Breath: Aphorisms and Essays, p. 81,* Agni Press, Jamaica, Queens, New York.

---. (1975) *Transformation-Night, Immortality-Dawn.* Agni Press, Jamaica, Queens, New York.

--- (1975) *The Sacred Fire, Act 2, Scene2; 4.* Agni Press, Jamaica, Queens, New York.

--- (1975) *The Sacred Fire, Act V1, Scene1; 3; p. 52,* reprinted 1998, Madal Bal, Zurich, Switzerland.

--- (1975) *The Sacred Fire, Act1, Scene2, p.14,* Agni Press, Jamaica, Queens, NY.

--- (1975) *I Need My Country: Beauty'sSoul, Section 1,* Agni Press, Jamaica, Queens, New York.

--- (1975) *I Love my Country: Purity's Body, Section1.* Agni Press, Jamaica, Queens, New York.

---. (1976) *Sri Chinmoy Speaks, Part 7, p. 22-25.* Agni Press, Jamaica, Queens, New York.

--- (1976) *Sri Chinmoy Speaks, Part 4,* Agni Press, Jamaica, Queens, New York.

---. (1976) *The Liberty Torch,* Agni Press, Jamaica, Queens, New York.

--- (1976) *The Bicentennial Flames at the United Nations,* Section 1. Agni Press, Jamaica, Queens, New York.

--- (1976) *Soulful Questions And Fruitful Answers,* Agni Press, Jamaica, Queens, NY.

--- (1976) *Dedication-drops, Poem 37,* Agni Press, Jamaica, Queens, New York.

--- (1976) *God the Supreme Musician,* Agni Press, Jamaica, Queens, New York.

--- (1976) *Dipti Nivas, (Cited in Disciple's Companion, Vol 2, P.202, 2006.)* Agni Press, Jamaica, Queens, New York,

--- (1977) *Aum Magazine, Vol 4, No 1, p.16,* Jamaica, Queens, New York.

--- (1977) *The Inner Journey, p. 46 – 47, Agni* Press, Jamaica, Queens, New York.

--- (1977) *Yoga and the Spiritual Life, p. 2; pp. 31-33,* Agni Press, Jamaica, Queens, New York.

--- (1977) *God, Avatars And Yogis,* Agni Press, Jamaica, Queens, New York.

--- (1978) *Flame Waves, Part 11, p. 25.* Agni Press, Jamaica, Queens, New York.

--- (1978) *Service Heroes, (Cited in Disciples Companion, P. 203).* Agni Press, Jamaica, Queens, New York.

--- (1978) *Philosopher-Thinkers: The Power-Towers of The Mind And Poet-Seers: The Fragrance-Hours of The Heart In The West,* Agni Press, Jamaica, Queens, New York.

--- (1979) Ten *Thousand Flower-Flames, Part 1,*Agni Press, Jamaica, Queens, New York.

--- (1980) The *Vision-Sky of California, Agni* Press, Jamaica, Queens, New York.

--- (1983) Ten *Thousand Flower- Flames, Part 98,* Agni Press, Jamaica, Queens, New York.

---. (1983) *Ten Thousand Flower- Flames, Part 61, No 6079 Agni* Press, Jamaica, Queens, New York.

---. (1983) *Ten Thousand Flower- Flames, Part 54, No 5400,* Agni Press, Jamaica, Queens, New York.

--- (1983) Ten *Thousand Flower- Flames, Part 66, No 6595,* Agni Press, Jamaica, Queens, New York.

--- (1983) *Ten Thousand Flower- Flames, Part 92,* Agni Press, Jamaica, Queens, New York.

--- (1984) *The Outer Running and the Inner Running, p.17, 19, 141, pp. 155-156, pp. 160-161,* Agni Press, Jamaica, Queens, New York.

--- (1984) *The Life of Sri Chinmoy, Part Two, p. 49,* Agni Press, Jamaica, Queens, NY.

--- (1985) *Beyond Within: A Philosophy for the Inner Life, p. 19, 20, 29, 39, pp. 44- 45, p. 47, 64, 69, 81, 441,* Agni Press, Jamaica, Queens, New York.

--- (1985) T*he Master and the Disciple, p. 3, 8, pp. 1-12; pp. 14-15, p. 28, 35, 47, 56, 60, 85,* Agni Press, Jamaica, Queens, New York.

--- (1987) *The Giver And The Receiver,* Agni Press, Jamaica, Queens, New York.

--- (1992) My *Father Shashi Kumar Ghose: Affection-Life Compassion-Heart Illumination-Mind, p. 5,* Agni Press, Jamaica, Queens, New York.

--- (1993) *Twenty-Seven Thousand Aspiration-Plants, part 193,* Agni Press, Jamaica, Queens, New York.

--- (1993) Aspiration-*Body, Illumination- Soul, Part 1,* Agni Press, Jamaica, Queens, New York.

--- (1993) *The Inner Role of the United Nations,*Agni Press, Jamaica, Queens, New York.

--- (1993) Meetings *With Luminaries In The Philippines,* Agni Press, Jamaica, Queens, New York.

--- (1994) *To the Streaming Tears of My Mother's Heart and to the Brimming Smiles of My Mother's Soul. p. 1, 5, 7, pp. 16 – 19; p. 23, 26, 35, 38.* Agni Press, Jamaica, Queens, New York.

--- (1994) *Disobedience Time is Up,* Agni Press, Jamaica, Queens, New York.

--- (1994) *My Heart Melody,* Agni Press, Jamaica, Queens, New York.

--- (1995) *Sri Chinmoy Answers, Part 6,* Agni Press, Jamaica, Queens, New York.

--- (1995) Sri *Chinmoy Answers, Part 3,* Agni Press, Jamaica, Queens, New York.

--- (1997) *God Is, p. 31,100, Aum Publications,* Jamaica, Queens, New York.

--- (1997) *Sri Chinmoy Answers, Part 8,* Agni Press, Jamaica, Queens, New York.

--- (1998) *My Brother Chitta, p. 12, 59, pp. 60-61, p. 63, 65.* Agni Press, Jamaica, Queens, New York.

--- (1998) The *Outer Running and the Inner Running, p.143,* Agni Press.

--- (1998) *Philosopher-Thinkers: The Power-Towers of the Mind and Poet-Seers: The Fragrance-Hours of the Heart in the West,* Agni Press, Jamaica, Queens, New York.

--- (1998) Seventy-*Seven Thousand Service- Trees, Part 6, Poem 5754,* Agni Press, Jamaica, Queens, New York.

--- (1999) Seventy-*Seven Thousand Service-Trees, Part 16, No. 15,555,* Agni Press, Jamaica, Queens, New York.

--- (1999) Seventy-*Seven Thousand Service-Trees, Part 13, No 12,777,* Agni Press. Jamaica, Queens, New York.

--- (1999) Sri *Chinmoy Answers, Part 18,* Agni Press, Jamaica, Queens, New York.

--- (2000) Sri *Chinmoy Answers, Part 26, Section 1,* Agni Press, Jamaica, Queens, New York.

--- (2001) Seventy-*Seven Thousand Service-Trees, Part 22, No. 21,362, (2001)* Agni Press, Jamaica, Queens, New York.

--- (2001) Sri *Chinmoy Answers, Part 14, Page 30, (2001),* Agni Press, Jamaica, Queens, New York.

--- (2003) The *Oneness of The Eastern Heart And The Western mind. Part. 1, p. 8, 60, 63, 71, 81, pp.96-97, p. 99, 100, 119, 130, 140, 163, 171, 303, 579,* Agni Press, Jamaica, Queens, New York.

--- (2003) Grace, *Page 34-34,* Aum Publications, Jamaica, Queens, NY.

--- (2004) *The Oneness of the Eastern Heart and the Western Mind, Part 2, p. 18, 77, 112, 149, 153, 173, 204, pp. 257-258, 355, 408, 464.* Agni Press, Jamaica, Queens, New York.

--- (2004) Oneness *of The Eastern Heart And The Western Mind, Vol 3, p. 30, 107, 112, 119, 149* Agni Press, Jamaica, Queens, New York.

--- . (2004) *Disciple's Companion, Vol 6, p.107, Agni* Press, Jamaica, Queens, New York.

--- . (2005) *The Master And The Circus Clown, p. 30, 31, 57,* Agni Press.

--- . (2005) *My Christmas-New Year Vacation-Aspiration-Prayers, Part 32,* Agni Press, Jamaica, Queens, New York.

--- (2006) Disciples *Companion, Vol 2, p. 10, Agni Press, Jamaica, Queen, New York.*

--- (2007) *My Christmas-New Year-Vacation-Aspiration-Prayers, Part 52, Aphorism 9,* Agni Press, Jamaica, Queens, New York.

--- (2008) *Behind the Curtain of Eternity, p. 26, 48, pp. 103-105,* Aum Publications, Jamaica, Queens, New York.

--- (2008) *A Day In The Life Of A Sri Chinmoy Disciple*, P. 10, 30, Agni Press, Jamaica, Queens, New York.

--- (2008) *The Life Of Sri Chinmoy*. Agni Press, Jamaica, Queens, New York.

--- (2009) Seventy-*seven Thousand Service-Trees, Part 50, No 49,284; 49, 209, 299*, Jamaica, Queens, New York. *Gill, R.S. (2004) Essence of Japji Sahib, pp. 43 – 44*. Delux Printers, Acton, UK. *Holy Bible: King James Version. Red Letter Edition. (John 3:6.)*

--- (Ephesians 2: V. 8- 9).

--- *(1 John 4: 16; 5:30).*

--- *(Matthew 6: V. 9-10; 33 -34). Maharaj, Nisargadatta Sri. (1986) I am That.* P. *49, 305*. Acorn Press, Durham, North Carolina.

Mata, Sri Daya, (1976) Only Love, p.16, Self-Realisation Fellowship, Los Angeles, California.

--- (1987) *Bhagavad Gita: The Song of God, P. 38, 80, 86; pp. 162-163,* Vedanta Press,

Ramdas, Sri, (1984) Thus Speaks Ramdas, Paragraph 63, Adandashram, India.

Vividishanananda Swami, *Gamghirananda Swami. (1975) For Seekers of God, 4th Edit.* Advaita Ashrama, Union Press, India.

Other Sources of References: http:/srichinmoylibrary.org; *http://us.srichinmoycentre.org*

A Meeting With Sri Chinmoy, Part1, Video. (2008) by MridungaSpettigue. Brochure: Jharna-Kala Fountain-Art. Courtesy Manifestation-Glow Press, Jamaica, NY.

William Collins Sons & Co, Ltd. (1966) Dictionary of The English Language. Collins Press.

Useful websites*: srichinmoy.org; nycmeditation.org; worldharmonyrun.org; srichinmoylibrary.com; srichinmoycentre.org; srichinmoy.org; srichinmoyraces.org; srichinmoycentre.org; heart-light.com.*

ABOUT THE AUTHOR

Manatita Kingsley Hutchinson

As a young boy growing up in the Caribbean, Manatita followed the religious life, and was very devout. Originally from Grenada, West Indies, Manatita moved to the UK in 1973, and later complimented his religious knowledge with the meditative life. Both were of great benefit to him.

Manatita found that change came quite suddenly. One day, while at home, he heard a sound as of something dropping through the flap of his letterbox. Going to the door, he found a book on the floor written about the meditative life. Manatita read this book from beginning to end and was totally transformed by the beauty and insights of that particular text. The book had a profound effect upon him, and from then onwards, he began to see life with much more wisdom, clarity and understanding.

Two weeks later, he found the telephone number to the Sri Chinmoy Centre in a small book called *Meditation: Paths to Tranquillity*. Manatita made a necessary phone call and walked into the Meditation Centre on October 1st, 1982. Today, 30 years later, he is still very much an active member of the Sri Chinmoy Centre, and an ardent disciple of the Master Sri Chinmoy.

Meditation, he says, has taught him a sense of purpose and the need to seek the Higher Ideals of life. He has learnt to look at humanity as if through the eyes of his Teacher, Sri Chinmoy, seeing the nobility, sacredness and universal oneness of all sentient and insentient life. Of supreme importance to Manatita, is the teaching of his Guruji of total and unconditional surrender to the will of the Supreme. Manatita gets a tremendous sense of inner joy in serving, and towards that end endeavours to offer in a small way to his brothers and sisters, Mankind, through many initiatives as taught by his beloved Guruji.